Praise for *The Trump Factor*

"Thomas works to rise above the fray of today's often corrosive political discourse to examine the business decisions of the era's most controversial real estate investor. With attention to both great successes and bruising failures, Thomas brings to bear his acumen as one of the industry's most prolific Real Estate Investment Trust and real estate analysts, giving readers the broadest look yet at the deals that have defined a brand."
-Dean Sam Chandan, Larry & Klara Silverstein Chair in Real Estate at the NYU SPS Schack Institute of Real Estate

"Brad Thomas has opened a new window for investors into the world of Real Estate Investment Trusts and real estate in the past couple years. With this book, Brad has provided an exhaustive and credible snapshot of Donald Trump's trophy real estate portfolio, and Mr. Trump's trials and tribulations while building his empire. The timing of Brad's book is especially eventful as Donald Trump takes the Republican baton to lead the Trump revolution to 'make America great again.' Mr. Trump's brand of vision, determination, professionalism and service are brought out clearly as Brad describes–property by property–when and how Donald Trump accomplished his success as a real estate entrepreneur."
- Mark Decker, Former Vice Chairman at BMO Capital Markets

"In *The Trump Factor*, Brad Thomas pulls back the curtain on Donald Trump's business empire in painstaking detail. He not only uses decades of experience in commercial real estate to provide a thorough accounting of the Trump real estate portfolio, but also offers valuable insights into how Donald Trump the entrepreneur built his name into an unstoppable multi-billion-dollar brand. The book provides one of the fairest and balanced looks at the legacy of Donald Trump to-date."
- Anthony Scaramucci, Managing Partner at Skybridge Capital

"In his new book, Brad Thomas examines the controversial yet successful Donald Trump. Thomas' financial acumen, coupled with his intensive research, provides insight into the key elements of Trump's business practices and the evolution of his real estate empire. A must read for anyone wanting to better understand the codependent factors of any real estate investment or the building of an empire outside of real estate."
- Jonathan Hipp, President & CEO at Calkain Companies

"In *The Trump Factor* Brad Thomas promises to pull back the curtain on Donald Trump and his vast real estate empire. Saying that Brad accomplished his goal by delivering a clear and detailed window into the Trump Real Estate Empire would be a gross understatement. If your only interest is learning about Donald Trump's vast real estate holdings, then the book is a must read. But the insights that resonated most loudly to me were the importance of seeing failure as opportunity and the tenacity to never give up, never give up. As I read through the book, it became crystal clear that real estate was not the only love that Brad Thomas and Donald Trump had in common. *The Trump Factor* also revealed that Donald Trump and Brad Thomas also share an uncompromising commitment to quality."
- Chuck Carnevale, Co-founder of F.A.S.T. Graphs™

"As a young person preparing to enter the world of business I read with excitement *The Art of the Deal*. Many of those principles I still use today. In *The Trump Factor*, Brad Thomas thoroughly examines each property and gives us a better understanding of how masterful Donald Trump is in business and marketing. This book gives me that same level of excitement I experienced many years ago when I opened up *The Art of the Deal*."
- Andre Bauer, 87th Lieutenant Governor of South Carolina and CNN commentator

THE
TRUMP FACTOR

UNLOCKING THE SECRETS BEHIND
THE TRUMP EMPIRE

BRAD THOMAS

A POST HILL PRESS BOOK

ISBN: 978-1-68261-265-1
ISBN (eBook): 978-1-68261-266-8

The Trump Factor:
Unlocking the Secrets Behind the Trump Empire
© 2016 by Brad Thomas

Cover Design by Quincy Alivio
Cover Photographs courtesy of Donald Trump

This book is intended to provide information to interested parties. The author takes no liability for the factual data provided and does not warrant the accuracy of the data provided by other third party sources. The author has used his best efforts to validate the content of this book and he takes no responsibility if information is published in error or by mistake.

Post Hill
PRESS

Post Hill Press
posthillpress.com

Published in the United States of America

TABLE OF CONTENTS

ACKNOWLEDGMENTS

First and foremost, I would like to thank God for giving me the opportunity to fail. It's through my own life failures that I have become a stronger husband, father, and investor.

Donald Trump has amassed enormous wealth with a portfolio made up of luxurious properties like Boardwalk and Park Place found in the board game, Monopoly. I never imagined that I would meet the legendary dealmaker, let alone write a book about his complex real estate endeavors and business acumen. But when I consider God's mighty omnipotent nature, it becomes clear that he is capable of moving human events in surprising ways.

"With man this is impossible, but with God all things are possible."
Matthew 19:26

Life is about taking risks and John Ortberg, author of *When The Game Is Over, It All Goes Back in the Box*, put it best by saying: "the greatest lesson comes at the end of the game."

Although *The Trump Factor* has given me an incredible platform to research Donald Trump's vast real estate portfolio, the biggest deal making lesson is that you can't take wealth when the game ends. In Ortberg's book (I highly recommend it), the author explains what really matters:

> *"It's not bad to play the game. It's not bad to be really good at it. It's not bad to be Master of the Board ... But there are always more rungs to climb, more money to be made, more deals to pull*

off. And the danger is that we forget to ask what really matters. We race around the board with shallow relationships, frenzied schedules, preoccupied souls. Being smart or strong does not protect you from this fate. In some ways, it makes the game more dangerous, for the temporary rewards you get from playing can lull you into pretending that the game will never end."

In addition to Donald Trump who has had a great influence in my life, there are so many people that I would like to thank for supporting me throughout my journey and I am grateful for all of them.

I'd like to start with my close friend, Brad Watt, who always encouraged me to be *better*, not *bitter*. I also want to thank my friends at *Seeking Alpha* who allowed me to publish my first article on December 2010 (over 5 million page views since then). *Seeking Alpha* has developed a great platform for investors and I am grateful for all 30,000 of my followers who have inspired me to become a better second-level thinker.

Chuck Carnevale, creator of *FAST Graphs* and also a fellow *Seeking Alpha* contributor, has also been an incredible mentor. His wisdom is far reaching and I'm thankful for his guidance in coaching me to become a true value investor and to think outside the box.

I have to thank my teachers, especially my college professor, Norman Scarborough, who inspired me to always seek value. I include my biblical teacher, Dr. D.J. Horton, who has not only inspired me to think about "what happens when the game is over" but also for educating my children on that most important lesson in life.

There are many CEOs that I must thank, not so much for content in this book, but for teaching me how to manage risk, arguably the most critical aspect of the investing process.

I have a long list of academic mentors. To name a few, many thanks to Dr. Brad Case, VP at NAREIT, Dr. Sam Chandan at NYU, Dr. Jan DeRoos at Cornell University, Chris Rousch at UNC, and Jonathon Morris at Georgetown University.

I want to thank my #1 research assistant and close friend, Michael Terry, as well as numerous college students including Chad Rukrigl,

Bryce Wied, Jing Jiang, Brian Zisin, Zhu Caroline, Jeroen Kerssens, and Stephen Cioromski.

I want to thank the people who encouraged me to write this book and those who took a look at the drafts. Here are the shout-outs: Debby Englander, Jessica Headrick, and Lauren Thomas.

I want to share my appreciation of the Trump Organization employees who were always helpful in delivering the highest level of service and cooperation. There are three employees that deserve a very special thanks: Rhona Graff, Meredith McIver, and Lili Amini, all very talented people and I am honored to have had the opportunity to work with them.

Finally, I want to thank my close family. My mother, Louise Thomas, who inspired me to never give up and she instilled in me the work ethic to always "keep pedaling." I want to thank my brother, Trey Thomas, who will always be my big brother (I always look up to my big bro!).

Last but not least, I want to thank my wife, Stephanie Thomas, for allowing me to invest our life savings into this book. I'm sure some will doubt me and suggest that Donald Trump paid me to write it, but my better-half knows the sacrifices better than anyone. I have also been truly blessed to be the father of five beautiful and amazing kids. AJ, Riley, Nicholas, Lexy, and Lauren. I am so proud of all of you and for teaching me how to play the game of life.

"We know that in all things God works for the good of those who love him, who have been called according to his purpose." Romans 8:28

INTRODUCTION

EXPOSING THE WONDERFUL WIZARD OF TRUMP

"Toto, I've a feeling we're not in Kansas anymore."
– Dorothy in *The Wizard of Oz*

You've picked up this book because you're either a fan of Donald Trump, or you're curious to read about whether or not he's actually worth billions. The truth is, this book should interest everyone, whether you love Trump or hate him. To put it bluntly, the purpose of this book is to provide the world with an inside look at the many mysteries behind Donald Trump.

Before I get started, I want to disclose that I'm a supporter of Trump. I don't agree with all of his political positions, but I started writing this book more than three years ago, and I never imagined that the content of my book would be as relevant as it is today.

To be clear, I have no interest in debating the merits of Trump as a presidential candidate. I am not a political writer and I have found that the best value for me, as a writer, is to focus on my circle of competence – commercial real estate.

When I met with Trump several years ago at his office, it became clear to me that the only way I was going to understand his businesses was to gain very close access to him and his people. I wanted to uncover exclusive details about him that would enable me to determine if this native New Yorker was really a master of the art of the deal.

I'm sure you remember watching the movie, *The Wizard of Oz*, when Toto, Dorothy's dog, pulled back the curtain to expose the human being who was thought to be the powerful and almighty Oz.

That is precisely the reason I decided to write this book – to pull back the curtain and provide readers with a true and accurate portrait of Donald Trump. Nobody, up until now, has taken the time (and money) to analyze every individual asset owned by Trump along with details on how he was able to build and then rebuild a business worth billions.

Dorothy realized in *The Wizard of Oz*, the real man behind the curtain was not made up of smoke and mirrors after all, but was ultimately a man as ordinary as you or me.

I assure you, I'm not sugar-coating Donald Trump. While I will provide you with great details of his vast real estate holdings, I am not going to paint a picture of a man who is superhuman. I do not know of any CEO who is infallible, especially those in the business of commercial real estate, where success is all about mitigating risk to generate returns.

To be successful in business, one must take risks. In life, we are all risk takers; the only difference between us is the degree in which we tolerate risk.

There is little argument that Donald Trump has taken greater risks in his life than many of us. Years ago when I was a shopping center developer, I borrowed hundreds of thousands of dollars to construct and lease buildings hoping that the risks I took would adequately compensate me. I made mistakes that cost me, but I also made hundreds of thousands of dollars, justifying my more than 20-year career in the real estate industry.

As the deals got bigger and bigger, so did my bank account. My tolerance for risk increased and I began feeling like I was Oz. Then, my curtain was pulled back. On paper, I was worth around $10 million, and that was in 2002. But I didn't control most of the wealth. Between the bankers and greedy partners, I wound up broke. The only reason I did not file for bankruptcy was because I could not afford to pay the bankruptcy attorney.

How could a 35-year old developer with five kids living in a $2 million house lose it all? Believe me, it happened. I have the battle scars to prove it.

All of us have defining moments in life. Mine came when I was sitting in the parking lot of a shopping center that I had previously developed. My wife asked me to go out and pick up some diapers and milk. I was sitting in the parking lot of the $15 million property that I once owned and I was thinking out loud, *"Why is it that I have just $20 in my pocket and the bag boys – in jobs that I helped created – are better off than me?"*

The answer: I made a bad bet. I had forgotten that the most important lesson in investing is to protect principal at all costs. I had become a gambler, not a developer. I was living off of high leverage with no diversification (I had one business partner then). The reality, although I never recognized it at the time, was that I was not managing risk.

As I further assessed my epiphany in the parking lot, I knew that I had to find a way to get back on top. With five kids, there was no time to waste, but I was broke.

As you may know, writing became my new career. I decided that I had a choice to make – either bag groceries – that was actually my first job – or begin writing on the subject of real estate. I did not want to write only about real estate, but also on the subject of managing risk within the real estate sector.

My passion for real estate is stronger than ever. I have a dedicated following of around 30,000 investors and many depend on me for research and recommendations. I don't have a degree from Wharton; I graduated from a small liberal arts college, Presbyterian College, and most of my education has been on the ground. Trial by error.

The most valuable education for me has been adversity. Because of the financial failures in my life, I have become a much stronger investor. It was painful to see the curtain ripped away from me but the end result was my becoming much more conservative and actually "sleeping well at night."

I've titled this book *The Trump Factor* because it will reveal the secrets behind the businesses and brand of Donald Trump. For the first time ever, I will provide readers with an accurate, unbiased, and hopefully entertaining book that will "pull back the curtain" and reveal to the critics, pundits, fellow journalists, and investors the many obscurities behind Donald J. Trump.

As the legendary investor Benjamin Graham once said:

"Adversity is bitter, but its uses may be sweet...in the end, we could count great compensations."

CHAPTER 1

THE RAISED NAIL GETS HAMMERED

*"In the business world, the rearview mirror is always
clearer than the windshield."*
– Warren Buffett

Donald Trump has been a surprise political headline of 2016, causing much debate and controversy. His name and company, however, have long been featured in business headlines, prompting much discussion in real estate, investment, and entertainment circles.

More than three years ago, I was fortunate enough to meet Trump and to spend some time with him and his executives at his properties. Initially, I considered myself lucky to gain some exposure to his huge empire and to have the opportunity to learn from his endeavors.

Gradually, I realized that many people – both in and out of the real estate business – wanted to know more about Trump. I was asked why the Trump brand traveled so successfully around the world. Other people wondered how much the Trump empire was really worth.

Frequently, people wanted to know why Trump seemed to have that ability to emerge from each deal, a little scathed, but ready for bigger and better ventures. Was Trump too big to fail?

I've pondered Trump's financial failures beginning with his risky investments in Trump Taj Mahal (1991), Trump Plaza (1992), and Trump Airlines (1992). How is it that Donald Trump never filed personal bankruptcy and was able to escape debtors' prison with barely a scratch?

As a developer, it's easy for me to recognize that the laws of leverage can enhance an investor's net worth by creating outsized returns. I'm a living and breathing example; that's precisely how I was able to turn my college debt into a small fortune worth around $10 million. However, like Donald Trump, I saw my net worth plummet as a result of high-interest debt and greed.

I don't consider myself a greedy person; instead, I consider greed an important element of the investing process. There's really nothing wrong with being greedy, especially when there's an opportunity to create a competitive advantage. The legendary investor Warren Buffett once said:

> *"Be fearful when others are greedy and greedy when others are fearful."*

Greed can be a positive tool, so long as it's tempered with discipline. How do investors obtain discipline? None of us are born with it, right? Jim Rohn famously said:

> *"We must all suffer one of two things: the pain of discipline or the pain of regret or disappointment."*

In my lifetime, I've experienced both discipline and disappointment. The two go hand-in-hand. Although my hard-working mother instilled in me the necessary discipline to know right from wrong, she never taught me how to become a disciplined investor. It took me years to recognize the balance required to become both a greedy *and* disciplined investor.

In fact, investing is really a process whereby you make money, lose money, rinse and repeat. At some point, the pain of regret becomes an advantage that precipitates the most important attribute of discipline. In other words, the secret to becoming an intelligent investor is really summed up in the word *discipline*.

One of my favorite investment writers is Zig Ziglar, who once wrote:

"Personal discipline, when it becomes a way of life in our personal, family, and career lives, will enable us to do some incredible things."

I remember reading these words in a book that my mother gave me when I graduated from high school, but it took me years to comprehend the true meaning of discipline, especially as an investor. It was the financial failures that forced me to become a more intelligent real estate investor.

When I think about Trump as an investor, I can understand the significance of his setbacks and his transformation from a high-risk player into a much more conservative one. Whether you've invested in one share of stock or in a vacation home, chances are you've experienced failure at some point. The reason nobody hears about it is because you aren't under the microscope, like Trump is today.

Think about it, what if you were investing millions of dollars into something, and the entire world was watching you? You turned $100 million into $1 billion, then $1 billion into $3 billion . . . and then the music stopped. All of a sudden you reach a fork in the road – do you suffer the pain of discipline or that of regret?

I can assure you, 99 percent of the population would suffer the pain of regret, but not Trump. He is in that one percent who has learned to steer away from the crowd and focus on becoming a greedy, yet more disciplined, investor.

Why is it that so many journalists focus on Trump's failures? The man has gone from real estate mogul, to celebrity, to presidential candidate, and is now being scrutinized by the media. There's been criticism and distortion about him, just as there are about most public figures. But the media has Trump's past all wrong. Because of my exclusive access to Trump, I believe I can provide an accurate view of the successes and failures of his business career.

First, I will address his failures. One of the biggest misconceptions, as it relates to Trump, is his bankruptcy history. For the record, Trump never filed personal bankruptcy. He could have – and perhaps should have – filed for bankruptcy, but he was able to stay afloat financially and stay out of debtor's prison.

Most individuals or corporations file bankruptcy for one reason: too much debt. Trump's first encounter in bankruptcy court was in 1991, when his casino, The Trump Taj Mahal, filed Chapter 11. Due to increased construction costs and high leverage, Trump's 42-story tower racked up over $1 billion in debt, forcing the company to restructure its balance sheet.

In 1988, Trump had acquired The Plaza Hotel in New York City for $390 million. By the time the Trump Taj Mahal had filed bankruptcy, The Plaza Hotel's debt load had risen to $550 million. As part of Trump's debt negotiation with his lenders, he was able to refinance The Plaza in exchange for giving up 49 percent of the equity in the prized hotel.

Keep in mind, Chapter 11 is an agreement approved by the court, so it simply gives the borrower time to work out the debt with the vendors and creditors. By 2004, Trump's casinos – including Trump Taj Mahal, Trump Marina, and Trump Plaza – had accrued over $1.8 billion in debt. By that time, Trump restricted his equity in the company from 47 percent to 27 percent.

The last bankruptcy was in 2009, and the trigger for this trip to court was related to the 2008 economic recession. Trump resigned as the company's chairman, and his corporate stake was further reduced to 10 percent.

Often in bankruptcy, creditors end up with pennies on the dollar and – in the case of Trump's casino businesses – the high-interest loans, or junk bonds, get virtually wiped out.

But that's the risk the investor makes. It is the banker's job to underwrite the bonds to ensure there's an adequate source of repayment. Trump was quoted, saying:

"First of all these lenders are not babies. They are killers. These are not the nice sweet little people you think."

Trump went on to say:

"Every company . . . every company virtually in Atlantic City has gone bankrupt."

At one point in time, Trump was personally responsible for around $900 million before he restricted his businesses. As you will learn in Chapter 14 of this book, Trump lost The Plaza, the airline and the casinos, but he didn't suffer any regret. Instead, he focused on rebuilding his empire. The difference in his blueprint going forward was that Trump learned to become a more disciplined investor. *Bloomberg* wrote about Trump:

"A new empire rose out of the wreckage of the first."

In this book I focus more on the *successes* than the *failures*. For the most part, the mainstream media has been critical of Donald Trump's oversized personality and willingness to speak his mind regardless of political correctness. It's important to understand how Trump has transformed from his earlier investments and has developed an overall strategy and philosophy that incorporates his personal insights with his business acumen; Trump's unique combination makes him a much more intelligent investor today.

The Trump Factor is about the one percent of the population, including Trump, which has ventured down the so-called road of risk. The true meaning of success is learning from mistakes and growing stronger. For the average person, it may be hard to understand the world of commercial real estate, but I hope that after reading this book you'll have a better understanding of how Trump was able to rise from the ashes and do, as Ziglar said, "some incredible things."

Why Focus on Failures? There will always be critics, and I'm certain the media will continue to focus on the failures, always looking for headlines and page views. For example, Jonathan R. Laing in *Barron's* wrote:

"Barron's isn't going to join many attempted media takedowns of Trump by unearthing new details about his business and personal life. They, so far, have only seemed to add to his celebrity and popularity. But we would like to revisit the incident dating back to the early-90s that we feel reflects on his character."

Russ Buettner and Charles V. Bagli with *The New York Times* said:

"But a close examination of regulatory reviews, court records and security filings by The New York Times leaves little doubt that Mr. Trump's casino business was a protracted failure."

Robert O'Harrow with *The Washington* Post wrote:

"Trump took extreme risks in a shaky economy, leveraged the Taj deal with high-cost debt, and ignored warnings that Atlantic City would not be able to attract enough gamblers to pay the bills, documents, and interviews show."

The Economist wrote:

"Information about Mr. Trump's business is sketchy. Yet his initiatives over the past decade have not been a wild financial success. But he has not yet created a great company, raised permanent capital on public markets, gone global or diversified very successfully."

Politico wrote:

"When I see he has only $300 million or so in debts, that's not a lot for a guy who claims to be a multi-billionaire. It says to me he doesn't own much of anything."

A friend in my hometown is worth around $1 billion and has a reputation for making money. However, if I told you what his name is most of you would not recognize it. Like Trump, I have followed my friend's success and failures for over two decades.

The difference between him and Donald Trump is that he flies under the radar. He has always kept a low profile and lives in a modest home in South Carolina. His name has no brand equity whatsoever. I'm certain that he can walk into any bank and get whatever he needs. I know that some of his real estate deals were failures, but you would never know about them because he lays low.

There's a common thread to these two billionaire investors and one that I find especially interesting. When they both encountered adversity, they did not run away from it. They kept moving forward, never taking their eyes off the prize.

Does the blueprint sound familiar? While some would mistake these billionaires as rude rather than confident, they were both transformed into shrewd businessmen. Both are battle-tested CEOs who have become successes because they learned from their mistakes. My friend and Trump both matured into intelligent investors who survived cycles of adversity, always learning and improving.

My billionaire friend once said, "The raised nail gets hammered," and I suppose he was referring to the avoidance of media attention because the bigger you are, the harder you fall. I'm sure my friend is perfectly content to stay out of the limelight.

But Trump doesn't mind it, in fact, he relishes it. I told Trump three years ago, "I will get it right." What I meant with that comment is that I intended to write the first book about Donald Trump focusing on an analysis of his empire. I have no interest in hammering him or praising him; my primary function is to analyze Donald Trump's blueprint and determine how much he really owns, how much debt he has, and how much is his actual net worth.

As I said, Trump could have easily taken an easier path by simply filing personal bankruptcy or suffering from his regrets. Instead, he opted to become a more disciplined investor. He took charge.

This book serves as a diary of my three-year journey. In my property-by-property analysis, I have uncovered some gems that are often overlooked. In fact, this book could be summed up as a master developer's blueprint of over five decades of value creation.

Donald Trump has a powerful combination of an architect's vision, financial genius, and unparalleled persuasiveness. These are only some of the tools he used to create a masterpiece business and an unparalleled one-man, one-name branding empire.

Never before has America, or the world, seen an individual so creative, so focused, and so determined to forge ahead regardless of the obstacles to create superb quality hotels, golf courses, condominiums, retail shops, and much more. Yet, his legacy lies in the family he tutors, empowers, and loves.

I'll now take you through the billionaire's blueprint so that you can see firsthand how the skilled investor was able to ignore the pundits and create vast sums of wealth by combining his passion for real property and his God-given intellectual property. These two forces are the catalysts that make Donald Trump the blueprint worth billions and what has inspired the world to recognize the immense power of *The Trump Factor*.

CHAPTER 2

THE FIFTH AVENUE CROWN JEWEL

"It's always good to be underestimated."
– Donald Trump

Critics were skeptical that Trump Tower would ever get built because many believed that Donald Trump didn't have the experience as a developer to complete such a large project. The proposed 68-story tower was deemed a pipe dream, and in 1976, Trump was an unproven 31-year-old real estate broker with a modest track record for deal-making.

Trump's visionary Fifth Avenue development was conceived as he roamed the New York City streets. He had just completed the successful redevelopment of the Commodore Hotel (discussed in Chapter 5) and his name was known only to a few bankers and associates whom he had met through his father, Fred Trump.

At that time, Trump had a net worth of less than $20 million, which was enough to entice a landowner to sign a contract for the land, but not enough to convince a bank to lend the enormous sum required to bankroll Trump's dream tower.

To make the project even more challenging, Trump's proposed development site had multiple owners and several leasehold agreements that made the odds less than favorable for completing the tower. He knew the project would be risky, but he also knew that the outsized returns would justify the unique set of challenges.

To say that Trump has an eye for spotting good real estate sites is an understatement.

Unlike any other developer that I have met (and that includes me), Trump has an incredible vision for selecting great locations. In his mind, barriers to entry don't exist as he embraces unconventional ideas by taking a mental picture and converting it into a virtual blueprint.

While most New York City developers would have proposed that the best use of the Trump Tower site would be a single-purpose building, Trump's vision included the currently non-conventional idea of multiple uses. Independent thinking is an integral part of Trump's natural talent of turning a visual image into an irreplaceable property and ultimately became his defining trademark.

According to his original salesperson, Louise Sunshine, Trump's endeavors never came easily. She said:

"Trump and I used to ride around in his car to identify the next project. I remember when we drove over to 57th [Street] and Fifth Avenue looking for a development site."

In *The Art of the Deal*, Trump wrote:

"For the time, I took an apartment in Manhattan and began walking the streets, the site that excited me the most was the eleven-story building at 57th [Street] and Fifth Avenue that housed Bonwit Teller. The main attraction was location, but in addition, it was on an unusually large piece of property. In my mind, that combination made it perhaps the greatest single piece of real estate in New York City. There was the potential to build a great building in a prime location."

In order to submit a development plan for Trump Tower, the young developer needed control of the site starting with the leasehold interest of the Bonwit Teller department store.

Bonwit Teller was owned by Genesco, which was founded in the late 1950's by W. Maxey Jarman. Over the years, Genesco became a conglomerate that owned retail chains such as Tiffany's and Henri Bendel as well.

Designed in 1929 for a store called Stewart & Company, the Bonwit Teller building was constructed to last decades as the exterior façade was a mix of limestone, bronze, platinum, and hammered aluminum. The original occupant, Stewart & Company, sold high-end woman's apparel typical of other luxury retailers along Fifth Avenue. In a blog by Joseph Kaminski, the author wrote:

"In a time when New York was the home of sophistication – full of polished and refined storefronts and shops that dedicated themselves to a department era of consumerism – the Fifth Avenue Bonwit Teller was the perfect representation of the time."

In a *New York Times* article, Chris Gray explained:

"Plain as the building might be, the entrance was like a spilled casket of gems: platinum, bronze, hammered aluminum, orange and yellow faience, and tinted glass backlighted at night. In 1929 American Architect magazine called it "a sparkling jewel in keeping with the character of the store."

Of course, Donald Trump was not as interested in the building on Fifth Avenue as he was the land underneath the twelve-story building. Trump first contacted Jarman in 1975 about buying the leasehold interest, but in 1978, just as Trump was hoping to lock-up the deal, Genesco began to experience financial troubles.

The Complexity of the Deal

After waiting for almost three years, Trump was relentless in his pursuit to contact Genesco and was able to get control of the site for a cost of $25 million. By optioning the property, Trump didn't risk any of his capital. He later explained:

"Without paying out a cent, we controlled the most fabulous location in all of New York City."

That was just the first piece of the puzzle. Trump then needed to get control of the parcel of land below the Bonwit building that was owned by Equitable Life Assurance Society. He had already established a business relationship with Equitable, as it was the lender for the Grand Hyatt project that was under construction a few blocks away.

Because of Trump's extensive Rolodex, he knew that he could connect the dots – he was already a partner in the Grand Hyatt so it would seem logical to extend the relationship into other business ventures, such as Trump Tower.

Consequently, the creative dealmaker was able to form a 50-50 joint venture with Equitable to contribute the land, making the project financeable for construction lending purposes. Without having to pay for the land, Trump was able to construct the project with very little equity.

The next thing Trump needed to do was buy the air rights from Tiffany's located on the corner of 57th Street and Fifth Avenue.

While most developers would have been content with designing and developing a midsize tower along Fifth Avenue, Trump was able to push the envelope to make his vision of "irreplaceability" the trademark for his successfully engineered blueprint. As Trump said:

"By purchasing the rights, I'd get something called merged zoning lot, which would allow me to build a much larger building."

Once again, Trump tapped into his contact list and called Walter Hoving, the president of Tiffany's. It was not that Trump needed the air rights; he could have delivered, in his words, "an uglier building." Yet, Trump convinced Hoving to assign the air rights for a sum of $5 million, and the deal was done on a handshake. Then Trump proceeded to build exactly what he wanted at the place he would later describe as the "Tiffany Corner." (Trump and his second wife later named one of his daughters Tiffany.)

Trump then needed a tiny 4,000 square foot strip that was critical to his plan. The city required this small parcel because there had to be a rear yard behind the proposed building.

He was able to extend the 25-year leased parcel by 75 years, allowing him to complete his land assemblage and begin to forge ahead with the design, construction, and eventual lease-up.

Louise Sunshine was Trump's number one lieutenant in the early years. She told us that she *"used to ride around in his car to identify the next deal."* She added, *"We were an invincible team."*

According to Sunshine, Trump Tower was a complicated configuration. The building's design has 28 surfaces that include a double-ceilinged six-level atrium. The irregular saw-tooth façade would create irreplaceable views for the most prestigious address in central Manhattan.

Trump closed the construction loan in 1979 and commenced construction with a projected cost of $200 million (excluding the land). The early critics were skeptical that Trump would succeed since the mixed-use design included spaces for retail (levels 0-4), office (levels 4-26), and residential (levels 27-68).

At the time, there were just a few condo sites, namely St. Tropez and Olympic Tower, but none offered the conveniences or upscale features that Trump was willing to provide. Trump stated:

"By adding a luxurious health club, fitness room, and other amenities, Trump Tower achieved the highest prices per square foot ever received for condominium units in New York City at the time it was completed."

While developing the landmark tower, Trump and his financial partner, Equitable Life, hired a general contractor to oversee construction. As the Bonwit Teller building was being demolished, the general contractor hired multiple sub-contractors to get the site into a pad-ready condition.

One of the subcontractors hired by Trump's general contractor was paid a fee of $775,000, to raze the Bonwit Teller's 10-story flagship department store.

Part of Trump's blueprint was seeking to hire the hardest-working laborers at the cheapest cost. At the time, construction workers were paid about $10 per hour, but Trump's general contractor was able to hire Polish immigrants for about $4 to $5 per hour.

Trump had ample funds to complete the project (remember, his partner was Equitable), but he wanted to make sure he could save as much money as possible on the front end because the interior improvements would be extravagant. Trump learned at an early age not to cut corners, but he also knew that he needed to stay on budget without sacrificing overall quality.

The demolition contractor later became insolvent and eventually filed a lawsuit in which the plaintiffs, who were undocumented Polish immigrants, argued that workers on the demolition site were cheated out of back wages and medical insurance funds.

Decades after Trump Tower opened, the demolition workers were still struggling to compel Trump to compensate a union's welfare funds which would increase pension and medical benefits for some of the Polish workers.

After numerous delays and appeals, the lawsuit was settled with no record of a fine paid by Trump. At one point, the projected penalty was around $4 million, but most of the fine was attributed to the plaintiff's lawyers. Trump claimed that he would have settled the case much earlier, but he insisted he had defended the lawsuit based on principle.

By admitting defeat, Trump recognizes that hundreds of potential plaintiffs would try suing him and compromise his tough "take no prisoners" mentality considered to be a defining leadership characteristic.

One of the lessons that I learned as a developer is that a contractor is only as good as a contract. Trump Tower was obviously built and is now worth hundreds of millions.

The Multi-Use Concept

Trump believed that the ground floor of a new building and three floors above could bring very high rents (in excess of $500 per square foot) from major retailers who coveted a Fifth Avenue address for a flagship site. He reasoned that the high floors with great views were ideal for the creation of luxury condos.

According to Louise Sunshine, Trump sold these units from $1,000 to $1,200 a square foot, with the best properties selling for $1,500 a square foot. While Trump was selling great convenience, he was also selling his trademark brand of success and ultra-luxury.

Within the iconic tower, Trump used the most luxurious finishes including rare Breccia Pernice stone that has an exquisite blend of rose, peach and pink. In addition, the building's interior design featured polished brass and an 80-foot high waterfall that cost an estimated $2 million to build. The building itself was constructed using concrete rather than steel beams, another trademark for Trump's premium blueprint and refusal to cut corners.

Trump knew he was selling the American dream, and the critics opted to cave in and admit the visionary creation – *The New York Times* proclaimed Trump Tower as *"A New York Blockbusters of Superior Design."*

In 2013, *The New York Times* interviewed Arthur W. Zeckendorf, a Trump clone who has prospered after following in Trump's footsteps, who explained that *"He (Trump) basically started the high-end condo business. I certainly followed him, and admired him."*

When asked what he learned from Trump, Zeckendorf replied:

"... building great condos is an art, and you really have to make the product the best out there."

There have been many famous buyers at Trump Tower, including Martina Navratilova, John Brown, Phyllis George, Regis Philbin, and Dick Clark; to name a few yet, the most prominent stakeholder is Trump himself.

By combining the top floors, Trump created a posh triplex with 53 rooms and a heavenly rooftop garden. At eighty feet in length, Trump's living room is fit for a king and the amenities include a waterfall, fountain, crystal chandeliers, carved ivory, and bronze – a look that's been described by the architect, John d'Alessio, as *"Louis XIV on LSD."*

So now, almost 40 years after Trump first dreamed of building on the legendary Tiffany corner, his multi-dimensional trophy is clearly worth multiples of millions. How many millions?

Let's Break It Down

First, keep in mind that New York City is the gold standard for commercial real estate. Trump's iconic trophy tower combining business and personal residences is nestled in the middle of one of the most expensive office and retail addresses in the world.

The residential units are always in demand and of course, at Trump Tower, there is no new supply. A one-bedroom unit purchased in 1979 would have gone for around $1,000 per square foot and units today are fetching around $3,000 per square foot. That means that residential units at Trump Tower have appreciated by over six percent per year over the last 39 years.

Excluding the sold condominium units in Trump Tower, the remaining commercial spaces, including twelve floors of office space and the 30,000 square foot penthouse, are the most valuable.

In addition, Trump purchased a 100-year-old leasehold interest in 1979, just behind Trump Tower, which houses the flagship Niketown store. Although not physically connected to Nike, Trump used the air rights for the Nike parcel to allow the developer to construct Trump Tower.

The 90,000 square foot store was previously occupied by Galeries Lafayette and in 1994 Nike signed a long-term lease with several five-year renewal options. The option expires in 2017 and Trump has been paying down the secured debt considerably (balance less than $20 million as of January 2016). The income generated from Nike is around $10.5 million annually and based on a cap rate of 3.5 percent, we estimate that the Nike deal is worth around $300 million.

There has been speculation that Nike could be relocating its flagship store but according to the recognized worldwide "Queen of Retail," Faith Hope Consolo, Chairman of Retail leasing with Douglas Elliman Real Estate, it's likely that Nike will stay put. *"Nike took a run at the GM building where Apple wanted to expand,"* Consolo said. However, retail brokers believe that Under Armour could move right into Nike's key location should the shoe company ever leave.

Donald Trump once said:

"If they (Nike) extend fine, if not, we will lease it. It's a great building. You know it was made out of steel."

The most valuable attribute of the Nike store and Trump Tower is the location of the real estate as Consolo explains:

"Trump Tower is the ultimate location. The value is in the location. This is 100% and nothing is bigger or better (than Trump Tower)."

Within Trump Tower, the retail tenants include Guess, Starbuck's, Mark Fisher Shoes, Tommy Hilfiger, and Gucci's flagship store. According to Consolo, retail lease prices along Fifth Avenue range from $3,500 to $4,000 per square foot. Trump also occupies space in the retail component for two dining options – Trump Grille and Trump Bar – and a kiosk that offers merchandise such as shirts, hats, and books.

Trump has four floors dedicated to his real estate businesses and Trump's daughter, Ivanka Trump, also occupies space for her fashion and accessory business.

Office tenants in Trump Tower include The Bank of China, offices of CONCACAF, the administrators of soccer in North and Central

America, headquarters of the 2016 Donald Trump Presidential Campaign (formerly the site of *The Apprentice*).

According to records, Trump is 100 percent owner of Trump Tower and the building is around 95 percent occupied (13,000 square feet vacant with asking rents of $125 per square foot).

Gucci, the anchor retail tenant, occupies 45,000 square feet and the Italian fashion house franchise recently increased its rent, making Trump Tower more valuable. We could not determine the precise rent that Gucci is paying but according to Bloomberg, Gucci was paying around $16.5 million back in 2010.

Several transactions have closed near Trump Tower including and based on these comparable sales; the 260,000 square feet of retail at $535 million and office space at $168 million at Trump Tower could fetch more than $700 million. To arrive at the value, we used the most recent retail comps near Fifth Avenue including closings at 522 Fifth Avenue ($10,400 per square foot) and 601 Fifth Avenue ($11,000 per square foot).

For the office space, we also looked at the latest comps where capitalization rates ranged from 3 percent to 4.5 percent and average closed transactions (provided by Real Capital Analytics) averaged $664 per square foot. We value the Trump Tower office space at the high-end of the range ($800 per square foot) given the superior location and amenities.

Combining the retail and office valuations for Trump Tower we arrived at a $703 million and then we added the value of the Trump residence ($100 million including the personal contents) and determined that the collection was worth $803 million.

Trump Tower was refinanced for $100 million in August 2012, allowing Trump to take a cash distribution of over $73 million. Since the loan is around four years old, we forecasted the current loan balance to be $95 million. The Nike building serves as collateral for bonds held by Trump worth $46.4 million and, since the loan is fully self-amortizing, we modeled the payoff at $10 million.

The Trump residence is harder to value because there simply are no true comps. In addition, the palace in the sky includes nearly all of

Trump's artwork, jewelry, and gold-plated bling. I spoke with several New York City residential brokers and they agreed that $100 million was a fair assessment given the irreplaceable real estate attributes and prestige of being the only building in the world located next to Tiffany's flagship store.

Trump once said: *"People are always surprised to hear that I almost named it Tiffany Tower."*

After deducting the conservative debt on Trump Tower, including the residence and Niketown, we arrive at a net worth of $864 million. That is considerably higher than many other media sources have reported and it validates the strength of the Trump brand. Owning high-quality real estate commands a premium and based on current market comparable sales, it's not hard to grasp that the trophy asset along Fifth Avenue, next to Tiffany's, is a crown jewel.

It took four decades for Trump to generate this wealth along Fifth Avenue while managing to ride out multiple recessions (and two divorces). The hard work and patience paid off handsomely and according to our pro-forma, Trump Tower and Niketown are generating well over $150 million annually. Once the new Nike & Gucci rent bumps kick-in and after the bond debt is retired, the cash flow should jump to over $175 million. This is clearly a great investment.

When Donald Trump built Trump Tower, he was creating a market for ultra-luxury real estate in Manhattan that had not previously existed. He had the foresight to believe that he could turn a worn-out department store into one of the most prestigious addresses in the world. Using one of his favorite real estate investing strategies, Trump combined an irreplaceable location with innovation and the end result was a portfolio of properties worth nearly one billion dollars.

The Trump Factor

TRUMP TOWER			
Properties	Sq. Ft.	$/Sq. Ft.	Totals
Retail Space	50,000	$10,700	$535,000,000
Office Space	210,000	$800	168,000,000
Trump Residence			100,000,000
Nike			300,000,000
Total			1,103,000,000
Debt (Trump Tower)			(100,000,000)
Debt (Nike town)			(10,000,000)
Trump Equity			$993,000,000

CHAPTER 3

TRUMP'S WALL STREET PIGGY BANK

"The way to make money is to buy when blood is running in the streets."
– John D. Rockefeller

orty Wall Street was built from 1928-1930 for the Bank of Manhattan Company. The developer, George Ohrstrom, started acquiring the land in 1928 and in May 1929 he began demolishing structures and laying the foundation for the office tower. The office tower was planned as a speculative tower with the bank taking a significant portion of the space.

Completed in 1930, this 1.3 million square foot, 72-story elegant skyscraper is one of Donald Trump's greatest accomplishments. It was designed in the Beaux Arts style and has many interesting footnotes in the history of New York City office towers.

After a mere year of record-breaking construction, including 93 days for erecting the whole building's steel frame, the building was officially opened on May 26, 1930, a day before its midtown rival.

Entered through bronze doors, underneath the sculpture "Oceanus" by Elie Nadelman, the building's interiors were a sumptuous undertaking. They included the two-story high banking hall with its marble decor and murals by Ezra Winter, the bank's boardroom (a replica of the Signers' Room in Philadelphia's Independence Hall), and wood-paneled executive offices with working fireplaces.

In the palatial surroundings, modernism was represented by the 43 high-speed elevators and the round observatory, the highest point in the city, reachable by stairs from the 69th floor.

During construction, 40 Wall was intended to be the tallest building in New York. A veritable race was on to build the "World's Tallest Building" and times were good.

Forty Wall *did* in fact become the World's Tallest Building in May of 1930 until Walter Chrysler, then building his eponymous skyscraper, pulled a now famous trick – he concealed his building's massive spire during construction in the lower floors until he was ready to see what his competitors, including the 40 Wall Street developers, had done. Once he was ready, Chrysler hoisted the spire to the top of his building, crowning it as the undisputable "World's Tallest Building" of the time.

The Depression of 1929 impacted many office towers in New York City and 40 Wall was not immune to the distress. But it was a double-whammy – 40 Wall's largest tenant, the Bank of Manhattan, was forced to reduce space. The building stood half-empty until the end of World War II when it attracted several notable tenants.

Like the Empire State Building, 40 Wall has also been hit by an aircraft. In May 1946, a Coast Guard transport plane hit the building in fog, killing the five people onboard. The building prospered up until the late 1980s when the Morgan Guaranty Bank exited the building for its new headquarters and left a 19,000 m² gap in the building's rentable space. At that time, it had only about 10 percent of its office space rented out.

A half-century after opening, 40 Wall became the subject of another infamous act. Brothers Joseph and Ralph Bernstein allegedly purchased the building as an investment.

In 1986, it was revealed that the brothers were acting on behalf of Ferdinand E. Marcos, the dictator President of the Philippines. Marcos was removed from power and his U.S. assets were frozen by the State Department. Thus, 40 Wall Street was in limbo for a decade thereafter.

Although the building changed hands twice after that, any plans for renovation (admittedly, quite ambitious too) were discarded as too costly. Trump smelled blood in the water and explained in *The Art of the Comeback*:

> *"Once I set my sights on it, I knew it would be mine ... The moment I laid eyes on it, I was mesmerized by its beauty and its splendor."*

Donald Trump bought 40 Wall, subject to a long-term ground lease in 1995, and started a massive, and badly needed, renovation in the building. Always on the lookout for a bargain, Donald Trump saw the building as a true opportunity to buy an iconic Wall Street skyscraper, in disrepair with but a handful of tenants, and execute a complete "turnaround."

A Real Estate Bargain

In fact, Trump was far ahead of his time with an idea to convert the top half of the building to residential use taking advantage of its vast, nearly unencumbered views of Manhattan. However, the expected cost to execute the conversion proved prohibitive. Undaunted, he proceeded instead with a well-planned and magnificently executed effort to renovate both the building itself and the mechanical systems, replacing all of the windows and bringing 40 Wall Street into the 20th century. His efforts paid off handsomely.

- There are two versions of what Trump actually paid for the building. The first is a figure of $1 million, an unreasonably low price for a 1.3 million square foot office tower.
- The second figure is $10 million, and at $7.69 per square foot, is still a ridiculously low metric.

However, the building was in such poor condition that a massive amount of capital was needed to bring it up to acceptable standards for potential high-end tenants. Trump was prepared and knew his organization's skill set was spot on. He found son, Don Junior, was the perfect ambassador to the leasing brokerage community which could market the property effectively.

It took much effort to execute the plan and no shortage of capital. The reports at the time showed that Donald Trump invested approximately $200 million ($153.84/square foot) into 40 Wall to make it a desirable building for future tenants and to meet the strict quality guidelines that Donald Trump sets forth for all his assets.

Even so, when adding this metric to the purchase price, the resulting investment is approximately $160/per square foot. Buildings in New York City have sold for nearly 7 to 8 times his investment in 40 Wall Street, making this single asset a veritable "home run" by creating what could be over $1 billion in value, above and beyond his costs.

But, to unlock value, 40 Wall needed income and Donald Trump's primary job was to enhance the value by bringing in top-notch tenants. After purchasing 40 Wall in 1995 and completing the much-needed renovations, the building was faced with nearly 50 percent of the leases in the rentable space expiring. Under normal conditions, that would not be a problem.

But this was in 2009, the country and New York City were in the depths of the Great Recession and nearly 600,000 square feet of leases were set to expire at 40 Wall. Trump Junior did exactly what his father had trained him to do – roll up his sleeves. In 2012, a story in the *Wall Street Journal* explained the tactical leasing strategy:

> *"The Trump Organization succeeded in leasing most of the empty space partly by reaching out to nontraditional Wall Street tenants such as Huron Consulting, the Harry Fox Agency, Duane Reade's corporate offices and engineering firms Weidlinger Associates and Leslie E. Robertson Associates."*

The article continues:

> *"Meanwhile, the Trump Organization was aggressive in giving tenants what they wanted: low rents and incentive packages. We had to bend a little bit more, and we could steal a tenant*

when we were in competition with a better building," said Jeffrey Lichtenberg, of Cushman & Wakefield, the landlord's agent.

The flurry of deals in the past six months marks the latest chapter in the story of 40 Wall, one of Trump's most successful investments. He purchased the Art Deco skyscraper for less than $10 million about 25 years ago when the city was struggling in the recession of the early 1990s.

The Downtown Revival

The new leases at 40 Wall reflect the metamorphosis of downtown. Creative and professional services tenants took more than 4.2 million square feet of new space between 2005 and the first half of 2011, according to a report by the Downtown Alliance. In contrast, financial services tenants took just 1.6 million square feet of new office space.

"We used to be much more reliant on Wall Street, but now it's more architecture firms, engineering firms," said Donald Trump Jr., 34-years-old, who is overseeing the leasing of the building for his father.

Office building investments typically follow one of two paths:

1. If purchased properly and well-located, they can create equity value by leasing-up vacant space, renovating the property to a higher standard, and charging more for space and managing the property effectively and efficiently; or
2. If the buyer overpays, most or all of the above-mentioned efforts will go toward making the building more valuable, but also making up for the added costs of overpaying; if the new owners, also called the "sponsors", do not have the expertise necessary to plan and execute an appropriate "game plan" for the property, or are unfamiliar with the market and submarket the property is located in, then they can rely on the myriad of professional services firms to guide them.

But professional services firms – leasing agents, marketing companies, website developers, and much more nowadays – are *not* owners. Most successful property services firms are familiar with the attributes and needs of a large building to help and support the owners to maximize value.

The ultimate decision about which way to go, what rents to charge, how to configure office space, what amenities must be in the building, and so much more, rests on the shoulders of the owner. Without this expertise at the ownership level, the likelihood of success is extremely low and the building may actually lease-up, but not at the maximum rent that could have been earned, therefore, the investment fails.

There are so many cases of wealthy individuals and organizations who wish to be in the "real estate business" yet they lack the expertise to effectively participate. Lenders are willing to lend on many properties based upon their current level of occupancy and level of reliable income. This reduces the amount of hard equity required to purchase and renovate an office building.

A lot of credit must go then, to the Trump Organization, and to Donald Trump himself, for the success of 40 Wall Street. It was purchased at a tough time in the cycle and faced even tougher times once it was ready for aggressive leasing to get to full occupancy. Downtown Manhattan was not at that time a "preferred" location for most office tenants. Financial firms were historically the likeliest candidates, but the financial sector literally blew up in 2009, leaving financial firms scrambling to survive, not looking for new office space.

Trump's "outside the box" thinking and leasing strategy paid off handsomely and son, Don Junior, executed the leasing plan, drawing kudos and compliments from the commercial leasing community – a tough group of people to begin with and certainly not known to be long on compliments.

If, in fact, Donald Trump had been able to execute his original concept of converting the top half of the building to residential use, he would have been far ahead of his time. Today, many examples of former office towers have been converted to residential use, quite successfully.

Currently, the area around 40 Wall Street is going through a true "renaissance" with new businesses cropping up frequently. Life in this part of town was predicated mainly around the hours of 9 am to 5 pm and then the workers loaded onto subways and buses to head to their homes. Now, many who work in lower Manhattan also live there, leave their offices and head to a nearby bar or restaurant, and then walk home.

The residential rental vacancy rate in Manhattan proper has hovered around 1 to 2 percent for several years. New development in the City is extremely difficult and takes a long time to "deliver" a new building – hence, residential rental supply simply cannot meet the demand, pushing rents for existing housing to all-time highs.

It has also pushed the boundaries of adjacent locations, making other boroughs more attractive to those seeking to rent, or purchase. New York City keeps growing as the *Millennials* do not want to live anywhere but smack in the city, a trend currently being seen in most other cities as well.

The high-dollar rental explosion just missed the property at 40 Wall Street. Regardless, the building is nearly 100 percent occupied and at strong rental rates with a good mix of tenants. Hopefully, it has an owner or manager who is both meticulous in the daily management of the property and in developing relationships with the buildings tenants.

This will pay dividends as tenant's leases expire and Trump can do what they do best – convince the tenant to stay and pay a higher rental rate for the identical space. Part of the success story for 40 Wall Street was in the transformational efforts like leasing and design. The other part is Donald Trump's shrewd investment acumen. Trump acquired 40 Wall from a Hong Kong group called The Kinson Company. As Trump recounts:

"The Kinson people had poured vast amounts of money into the building but into things you don't see – air conditioning, mechanical systems, and so on."

With costs piling up for Kinson, Trump was able to financially engineer the deal by paying the distressed owner a modest profit (as I said our sources suggest it was either $1 million or $10 million) and assume the construction liens that were piling up (that may explain the difference in the $1 million or $10 million price tag).

But it was not so much Trump's savvy negotiating skills that made this unique asset so valuable, it was the fact that the billionaire developer knew that he could unlock substantial value by renegotiating the underlying ground lease with the ownership group in Germany.

As Trump was negotiating the acquisition of the leasehold property he was simultaneously negotiating with the landowner to extend the sixty-three-year lease to a two-hundred-year ground lease. This allowed Trump to seek more favorable lending terms for the building and also ensure future Trump generations that the underlying cash flows would last.

Trump changed the name of the building from 40 Wall into Trump Building at 40 Wall. The building is easily visible from Wall Street and directly across from the New York Stock Exchange. Now everyone on Wall Street knows where to find Trump's iconic tower.

Tenants in 40 Wall include Country-Wide Insurance (108,241 square feet), Green Ivy School (86,350 square feet), Haks Engineering (69,916 square feet), Duane Reade (77,810 square feet), and others. Current rents for office space in the area range from $40 to $60 per square foot.

The 86-year-old Manhattan skyscraper has also filled up all of its ground-level retail space with Duane Reade occupying a retail store on two levels of the building. The structure is 95 percent occupied and estimates show the building generates around $25 million per year in cash flow.

Forecasts are based on industry-recognized expense deductions and estimates for the annual ground lease payment. There are an additional 50,000 square feet that could be leased to add another two million or so to the bottom line.

A Current Assessment

Trump refinanced 40 Wall Street in July 2015 with Ladder Commercial, a leading commercial mortgage REIT and also a lender to several other Trump-owned buildings. There are three loans – all senior secured – that total $170 million with a maturity date of July 2025. The loans are nonrecourse to Trump individually. As Jim Costello with *Real Capital Analytics* explains:

"There are three loans we know of on 40 Wall Street totaling $160m. These loans came through the CMBS market and as such some information on the appraised value of this asset also came through. At the time of financing, this asset was put at a value of $540m. The market has moved on from there, it is probably worth more today. Still, even with a potentially low estimate of the value of the asset, it would put the LTV for this asset at 30%, a conservative level of debt."

Trump could have easily increased his leverage on 40 Wall, but Costello clarifies:

"Suppose we hit another downturn in the market just as bad as the one seen in 2008-2009. The Moody's/RCA CPPI ™ measures commercial property prices in the US and posted a cumulative 40% decline between October of 2007 and January of 2010. A $540m investment made in October of 2007 would, on average, only been worth $324m by January of 2010. Still, if the asset had only $160 m in debt to repay, then by the trough of the market the asset would still be worth more than the outstanding debt."

The amount of leverage on an asset is captured in the Loan to Value (LTV) measure. New purchases of commercial assets in Q1'16 have had LTVs averaging 65 percent. Back before the Global Financial Crisis, this measure averaged 70 percent nationally, but some high-flying investors purchased assets with LTVs in the high 90 percent range. Those investors needed both asset value growth and income growth to make these investments successful. When the market turned, there was little choice but to throw the keys to the lender.

In a market where asset values are growing, it can be easy to pay off a loan if one needs to sell an asset for any reason. In a downturn, however, if an investor has too much debt on an asset, one may quickly end up owing more than the fundamental worth of that asset.

Using our estimated cash flow model and our cost approach model, we estimate the value of 40 Wall to be $565 million. The income estimated is based upon office rent income of around $40 to $45 per square foot and we have used a capitalization rate of 4.7 percent (based on the most recent transactions closed in the immediate area).

We estimate Trump's equity in 40 Wall Street at $400 million and we have arrived at this estimate by subtracting around $165 million in debt (the loan closed in 2015 so we assume a principal reduction of at least $5 million) from the valuation of $565 million. We estimate that Trump's cash flow (after debt service) on 40 Wall is around $25 million per year.

Note: We also factored in the annual lease payments that Trump pays the landowner of $1.65 million (according to *Bloomberg*).

In addition, 40 Wall pays Trump's real estate management business gross revenue of around one million annually. That money goes into the company's asset management business to help pay for staff at The Trump Organization.

Throughout his successes and failures, John D. Rockefeller has always been viewed as a savvy businessman and somewhat of a cutthroat capitalist who ruthlessly disposed of and acquired competitors to make his fortune. Similarly, Donald Trump has proven his success by taking advantage of botched pricing and cutting costs while increasing efficiency.

Trump 40 Wall is a case study in creating value and Donald Trump's $565 million Wall Street Piggy Bank generates almost $25 million per year in free cash flow.

Trump should continue to see his equity accumulate in 40 Wall as the downtown financial district of New York City undergoes a robust expansion as explained by Sam Chandan, PhD, Associate Dean at NYU's Schack Institute of Real Estate:

> *"For many investors, Lower Manhattan had been viewed historically as a second-best alternative to Midtown. That notion was reflected in leasing activity and prices for downtown buildings that often traded at a significant discount. Many investors who acquired properties while this view held sway have subsequently booked impressive returns, particularly over the last few years as Lower Manhattan's population has burgeoned and the vision for the World Trade Center site has taken shape."*

The Trump Factor

TRUMP 40 WALL			
Properties	Sq. Ft.	$/Sq. Ft.	Totals
Office/Retail Tower	1,300,000	$434.62	$565,000,000
Total			565,000,000
Debt			(165,000,000)
Trump Equity			$400,000,000

CHAPTER 4

THE OFTEN OVERLOOKED TROPHIES

*"I wasn't satisfied just to earn a good living.
I was looking to make a statement."*
– Donald Trump

Rarely can anyone identify a real estate professional as prolific and intense as Donald Trump himself, but Steve Roth, founder, Chairman, and CEO of Vornado Realty Trust (NYSE: VNO) is that person.

From a fundamental idea 40 years ago, he has created one of America's greatest public real estate empires. The company he built is now traded on the New York Stock Exchange and has a total capitalized value of well over $30 billion.

Steve Roth differs from Donald Trump in his public persona; it is a virtually non-existent one. I once tried to speak with him on an elevator in New York and he shrugged me off (maybe because I was bearish on the high-priced shares of his REIT).

He does appear frequently at key real estate industry events, usually as the main speaker, and always has an interesting perspective on the world of real estate. He doesn't venture off into politics or other subjects outside of commercial property. He may go as far as touching on the interest rate environment and the Federal Reserve but that's about it.

Otherwise, the two men are singularly focused on a common theme: acquire, develop, lease, and manage the best real estate possible. In this regard, both have succeeded.

Intersection of the Two Greats

Given this common passion, it was inevitable that Steve Roth and Donald Trump would bump into one another in a prospective transaction. That did occur many years ago when both decided to acquire stakes in Alexander's, a retailer based in Manhattan that was having trouble.

It wasn't the dresses or suits that they had their eyes on; it was the real estate that Alexander's owned for its retail stores. The flagship Alexander's commanded a near full city block at 58th street and Lexington Avenue, a prime development site that both Roth and Trump lusted over.

The potential density and height of an office tower on that prime location had both men salivating over finding a way to get it under their control. By acquiring shares in the publicly held Alexander's, they made their move. Who won?

Before revealing the scorecard, let's understand one thing: real estate is a very long term business and new skyscrapers are not built in a day. In fact, the new, elegant and premier building that ultimately rose on the Alexander's site took a full 3.5 years to build and lease. In the end, the tower became the global headquarters for *Bloomberg* and the condominium residences there sold for record-breaking prices.

The Long Saga Begins

Donald Trump acquired 27 percent interest in Alexander's in 1989, and Steve Roth purchased about 29 percent of the outstanding shares. Now this 2 percent delta wasn't the difference that won the rights to the site; rather, it was the finality of the exuberant 1980s that ended it.

Donald Trump had amassed an enviable real estate portfolio by that time, but along with it, he had accumulated an undesirable amount of debt. It was the debt that became his day-to-day cross to bear and he eventually acceded the battle over Alexander's to Roth; it was an unequal exchange agreed to be in Roth's favor.

This one act of pleasantry seemed to have set the stage for long-term mutual respect between these two men as they forged ahead and eventually built two of America's greatest real estate empires.

Cordially Competing Forces

In 1998, General Motors owned its eponymous office tower in Manhattan. The company decided to sell it and a bidding war erupted between Donald Trump and Roth as well as a cacophony of other bidders. Trump was the victor with his purchase of nearly $900 million, this time outdoing Roth.

Trump sold the tower five years later and collected a huge profit. Had he actually held it longer, he would have made even more money since the property is an iconic trophy asset of immense proportions – think of the grand appeal of the Apple Store in its magnificent glass enclosure *if* it only happened to be on street level – and continues to rise in value. Boston Properties, Inc. (NYSE: BXP) acquired the GM building for nearly $3 billion many years later.

In the small world of Manhattan commercial real estate, deals are generally made through relationships. Both successful and failed deals provide the opportunity for people to build these relationships because they spend time together. Sometimes the oddest couples end up working jointly on a deal.

West Side Yards – Riverside South

If you look at an aerial map of Manhattan, the lower left side near the Hudson River has a huge swath of vacant and underused land. Penn Central Railroad owned the site and eventually sold it to Donald Trump for $115 million and much of it was debt.

This transaction dates back to 1985, the veritable high watermark of the overly enthusiastic '80s. With 77 acres of flat land on which to build, it was originally named "Television City" with the possibility that the National Broadcasting Company (NBC) would move their global headquarters to the site. It eventually became "Trump City" with a potential density of 18 million square feet.

While Trump City didn't represent an untenable level of debt itself, Trump was out making larger deals and piling up massive levels of debt elsewhere. Eventually, the 1980s became the 1990s and things settled down. Trump was beginning to default on several loans and began looking for a way to salvage his empire.

Asian Investors – The Plaza Hotel

An unrelated meeting with a group of wealthy Asian investors who traveled to New York with high hopes of acquiring The Plaza Hotel from Donald Trump occurred in 1989.

During this meeting, Trump shifted the focus from the Plaza Hotel to Riverside South telling the Asian investors that it was the *"greatest undeveloped parcel of land in the world."*

After 90 minutes of hearing how successful the site could become, the investors decided to acquire it from Trump and keep him in the deal as a minority partner with 30 percent interest. When the Asian investor group decided years later to sell the entire project for an enormous profit to The Carlyle Group and a local New York developer, Trump balked at the price saying he could have gotten them much more. Remember, he still owned a 30 percent stake, which was effectively a gift from the Asian group.

Instead of confronting Donald Trump, the Asian group took the proceeds from the sale and purchased two other projects, one in San Francisco and the other at 1290 6th Avenue in New York City, a massive 2.1 million square foot office tower. They agreed to keep Donald Trump in the deal at the 30 percent continued interest from Riverside South. Eventually, the Asian investor group decided to sell their majority 70 percent interest in 1290 6th to Vornado Realty Trust, led by none other than Steve Roth.

Partners at Last

What comes around goes around. After years of dueling for deals, Trump and Roth finally land on the same page as the two legendary dealmakers are now partners in two massive skyscrapers.

Valuing Trump's equity stake within the two Vornado buildings is easier because we have access to the Real Estate Investment Trust's (REIT) publicly-available filings. In 2007, Vornado acquired the 70 percent stake in 1290 6th Avenue of the Americas for $1.807 billion. The 2.1 million square foot office tower is over 99 percent leased with a roster of high-quality tenants like Cushman & Wakefield, Bryan Cave, LLP, and Sovereign Bank. As of 2016, Vornado signed a 20-year lease with Neuberger Berman Group to occupy 355,000 square feet.

In 2012, Vornado refinanced the building by taking out a $950 million loan that matures in 2022. The interest rate on the secured debt is 3.34 percent. It appears that the partnership refinanced the property in 2012 replacing the previous loan of around $400 million. We assume that Trump took out 30 percent of the loan proceeds or around $150 million (we're adding that to our cash account column).

In Chapter 2 (Trump Tower), we used office sales comps along Fifth Avenue of roughly $800 per square foot (for Trump Tower) and using the same comparable data, we believe that 1290 6th Avenue should also be valued at the high-end of the range, and also reflecting appreciation of at least 25 percent since Vornado purchased the trophy in 2007. Thus, we value the 2.0 million square foot building at $1.6 billion.

Subtracting the secured debt, we arrive at property-level equity of $650 million, of which Trump's equity is valued at $195 million.

As referenced above, Vornado also acquired a controlling interest in 555 California Avenue in 2007. This is Trump's only investment in San Francisco where the landmark office tower enjoys occupancy of over 98 percent. The building was constructed in 1922 and, in addition to the anchor tenant, Bank of America, the building is also home to Goldman Sachs and Sidley Austin, to name a few. Microsoft moved into the property in 2014 where it occupies 50,000 square feet and pays $62 per square foot in rent.

Vornado acquired the high-rise for $575 million and adjusting for appreciation, we believe the 1.8 million square foot tower is worth $1.3 billion. Vornado also refinanced the building by taking out a loan in the amount of $600 million in 2012. The current balance on the loan is $589 million and the value of the partnership is estimated at $711 million, of which Trump's equity is $213 million.

Other Low Hanging Fruit

Trump Tower and 40 Wall are two of the most recognized office towers in New York owned by Donald Trump, but many are not aware of the other vast holdings in his Manhattan building collection.

Many do not know that Trump used to own the land underneath one of the most well-known skyscrapers in the world, the Empire State Building. As referenced in Chapter 3 (40 Wall) Trump understands the role that ground leases serve and how to exploit value by either extending leases for more favorable debt terms or by purchasing the land outright to squeeze the ground lessor.

In 1961, Harry B. Helmsley, Lawrence A. Wein, and his son-in-law Peter Malkin bought the Empire State Building for $65 million in a syndication deal. To structure the deal, the owners created an entity to own the building and another entity that owned the land, simultaneously selling the land to Prudential Insurance.

Thirty years later, in 1991, according to *The New York Times*, Prudential sold the land for $42 million to an investor who was secretly acting on behalf of Hideki Yokoi, a Japanese businessman. It was not a good deal for Yokoi since the income being generated was less than 1 percent. Yokoi's daughter, Kiiko Nakahara, decided to forge a partnership with Trump to force a better outcome.

A lawsuit followed and after a few years of litigation, Trump was able to squeeze out a profit of around $15 million (some sources believed it was less and *The New York Times* claimed the profit for Trump was $6.25 million).

Donald Trump has been known for decades as the premier developer in New York City and it is because of his reputation as a dealmaker that he gets a first look at many projects that bear meaningful fruit. Let's face it, Trump knows New York City's real estate market better than anybody and, accordingly, he has been able to increase his net worth by picking off the low hanging fruit.

In the mid-80s, Donald Trump was planning to construct a new residential tower at 106 Central Park South. He met considerable opposition as entrenched tenants living in the 38-story midrise complained that they wanted to remain living in the rent-regulated apartments. One tenant at the time, John Moore, argued:

"I don't need Donald Trump's glitz on the outside of my building."

The battle eventually ended and Trump settled to renovate the property as condominiums in which he renamed 106 Central Park South as Trump Parc: The Condominium.

To monetize his hard work, Trump had to convince many of the tenants to become buyers. That was difficult since 43 out of 80 apartments were occupied by rent-regulated tenants, most paying below market value. The remaining units sold quickly and Trump was able to recapture most of his initial investment at prices ranging from $220,000 to $1.9 million.

In *The Art of the Deal*, Trump explained how he:

"... put the apartments on the market in November 1986. Within eight months, 80 percent had sold—nearly 270 apartments. One individual bought seven, for a total of $22 million. When the building sells out—in all likelihood before a single person has moved in—I'll have grossed in excess of $240 million. And that's before I do anything more with 100 Central Park South and the stores across the street."

The extravagant entrance at Central Park South establishes its place at Central Park and was transformed to include restoration of the existing masonry walls and enormous windows. The limestone base of the building was added to house retail space. The lobby boasts Trump's signature style with marble, polished granite, and lush landscaping.

According to our sources, Trump still owns 19 units (out of 340) at Trump Parc as well as the ground-level retail stores. Trump Parc has

Central Park as its front yard and is steps away from upscale dining and shopping on Park and Fifth Avenues, MoMa, Columbus Circle, and Rockefeller Center. This is full-service, white-glove luxury living with historical relevance, elegant innovation, and only steps away from everything that defines Midtown Manhattan.

Trump bought the Trump Parc property in 1988, along with a smaller building known as Trump Parc East (100 Central Park South), another luxury residential mid-rise, formerly the St. Moritz Hotel. Trump Parc East is another example of Donald Trump's many "white glove" successes in New York City. This project is smaller than Trump Parc and the billionaire still owns thirteen apartments that, according to *Bloomberg*, could fetch around $30 million "on the open market."

Donald Trump bought The Delmonico Hotel located at 59th street and Park Avenue in 2001 for $115 million. Similar to Trump Parc and Trump Park East the billionaire decided to convert the iconic 35-story hotel into 120 luxury condos. The Upper East Side is synonymous with elegance and upscale living and Donald Trump recognized that he could transform the property into a profitable deal.

The Delmonico Hotel was built in the late 1920s and Trump created 120 luxury homes, ranging in size from one to seven bedrooms. The building, constructed of hand-laid brick with ivory terra-cotta trim, underwent a painstaking renovation that included adding 12,000 square feet of floor space and redesigning some of the building's terraces into gorgeous, glass greenhouses.

Trump renamed the project Trump Park Avenue (502 Park Avenue) and the hotel rooms were transformed into gracious and luxurious homes containing the finest in technology and premium details. Reportedly, the renovation's total cost was $100 million.

Private elevators open onto the 20th floor and beginning there are 12 full-floor apartments. They range in size from over 4,000 to 7,000 square feet. Floors 31 through 32 hold the penthouse duplex that has a 17-foot aerie with vaulted ceilings, arched windows, and very large terraces.

Trump Park Avenue is a landmark architectural marvel in one of the Upper East Side's loveliest streets with Central Park as its backyard, international boutique shopping, and world-renown restaurants, as well as five-star hotels such as the Four Seasons and The Plaza nearby. MoMA, Frick Mansion, and the Whitney Museum are within walking distance, as are some of Manhattan's most prestigious public and private schools.

According to *Bloomberg*, Trump still owns 20 condo units at Trump Park Avenue and the combined value is around $200 million.

In addition to the significant equity Trump has within his vast portfolio, many are not aware of the little gems that are hidden along roadsides in New York City. Over the decades, Trump sold off hundreds of condominiums (except for around $230 million noted above – 100 Central Park South and 502 Park Avenue) but he managed to retain equity in several street-level buildings that could be worth as much as $100 million.

In summary, we have uncovered substantial value in the "often overlooked" properties that are not easily recognizable. Trump's partnership with Vornado boosts the billionaire's net worth by over $800 million and the nuggets scattered across New York City streets provide another $330 million to the bottom line. Collectively, these crumbs add up to a substantial piece of Donald Trump's growing empire – in which the "often overlooked" properties add another $1.131 billion to the billionaire's bottom line.

The Trump Factor

OVERLOOKED PROPERTIES		
Properties	Details	Totals
1290 6th Avenue		$195,000,000
555 California Avenue		213,000,000
502 Park Avenue		200,000,000
100 Central Park South		30,000,000
Various (NYC)		100,000,000
Total		738,000,000
Equity		$738,000,000

CHAPTER 5

TRUMP HOTELS

"Success seems to be connected with action. Successful people keep moving. They make mistakes, but they don't quit."
– Conrad Hilton

Donald Trump once said, "Real estate is part of my DNA" and he meant it. His grandfather, Frederick Drumpf, was born in Kallstadt, Germany, back in 1869. At the age of sixteen, he decided to make his fortune in the United States so he left his mother a note and sailed aboard the SS Eider into New York City.

With just a suitcase and a passion for succeeding, Drumpf became a naturalized U.S. citizen and changed his name from Frederick to Fred Trump. In 1891, at the age of twenty-two and after hearing about the fortunes being made out west, Trump journeyed to Seattle hoping to make it big in the gold business. With his life savings – just a few hundred dollars – Trump purchased a restaurant called the Poodle Dog that he later renamed Dairy Restaurant.

In just two years, Trump made a quick profit selling the restaurant and decided to travel to Monte Cristo, Washington. The area was known for its mineral resources and prospectors were flocking to the small town in hopes of making a fortune in gold. Before leaving Seattle, Trump made his first real estate investment – he paid $200 for 40 acres in the Pine Lake Plateau.

When he arrived in Monte Cristo he made another investment. Instead of buying the fee-simple interest in a parcel of land, he filed what's referred to as a Gold placer claim that provided mineral rights to the land without having to pay for it. Trump never mined for gold; instead, he built a hotel for the miners that became very successful. He later purchased the land in 1894. Two years later, he was elected to the office of Justice for the Peace by a 32 to 5 margin.

Sound familiar? Perhaps politics is also part of Donald Trump's "DNA." Trump sold off most of his property in Monte Cristo a few weeks later and moved back to Seattle to open a new restaurant venture. He then traveled around quite a bit, opening up other hotels and restaurants and eventually in 1901, he decided to move back to his home country. A year later, he reunited with his childhood girlfriend, Elizabeth Christ, and they were married on August 26, 1902.

Trump and his new bride moved back to New York, but only 16 years later in 1918, he unexpectedly died at the age of 49. Before he died, he was living in Queens where he had amassed around $500,000 in today's dollars.

Continuing the Legacy

Reflecting on Donald Trump's heritage – his grandfather was a German immigrant – it's clear to see that there is a common thread that runs deep into the roots of the Trump blueprint. The Trump name is synonymous with hard work and real estate.

One of the biggest misconceptions relating to Donald Trump is that he was born with a silver spoon, but that could not be further from the truth.

He did have parents and grandparents who helped him financially, but more importantly, his closest kin taught him the meaning of hard work. Frederick Trump was the epitome of a man driven by a strong work ethic and was able to turn two nickels into a small fortune by the age of 40.

Who would have known that Donald Trump's grandfather would also serve as the inspiration for a hotel business that would scale the globe? Much like the game of Monopoly, the secret to winning is starting small, investing in lesser houses and eventually upgrading to greater hotels. That's how Fred Trump amassed his fortune, but Donald Trump did not play by the same set of rules.

When Donald Trump was just 27-years-old and only a few years out of college, he decided to bypass the smaller deals and jump right into the big leagues of New York City.

He was not exactly battle-tested at the time so his first major deal would not only provide credibility in the future, but also valuable experience that would spark a lifetime of self-assurance. This first large real estate transaction was to convert the rundown Commodore Hotel next to Grand Central Station into the Grand Hyatt Hotel.

His dream, or more precisely his visual blueprint, was to purchase one of the most distressed buildings in New York City and turn it into one of the most successful. Using the Monopoly example, Trump wanted to take the cheapest property – Baltic Avenue – and turn it into Boardwalk, the most luxurious.

Clearing the Way

But there were layers of hurdles that Trump needed to clear and many were out of his control. To start with, New York City was in trouble. According to Arthur W. Zeckendorf:

"The city was going bust in the 1970s. Everyone was leaving. Corporations were moving out."

Steve Cuozzo with *The New York Post* describes New York City in the 1970's:

"No matter how many times they watch "Taxi Driver," younger New Yorkers and older ones who arrived recently have no idea of what the city was actually like in the mid-1970s through the mid-'90s. Notwithstanding Studio 54 and a short-lived Wall Street boom, the metropolis was reeling. Rampant street crime, AIDS, corporate flight and physical decay brought confidence to an all-time low."

Trump's net worth at the time was just a few million and his plan was to convert the Commodore Hotel into a 32-story first-class convention hotel containing 1,400 rooms. It would be the largest hotel since the New York Hilton was built 25 years earlier.

One of Trump's key lieutenants then, an attorney by the name of George Ross said:

"When 27-year old Donald Trump explained the grandiose idea to me during our first meeting, I told him that based on existing conditions he was chasing an impossible dream that would never happen."

According to Ross, Trump would have to win over "major concessions" from the landowner (Penn Central), New York City, the State of New York, lenders, the hotel chain, and existing tenants. Just one of these concerns would have been enough for an enterprising young developer to strike out, but Trump never quit swinging for the fences.

"Many of his brainstorms were ahead of their time," according to Cuozzo; yet Trump never gave up. And in 1980 he completely rebuilt and modernized the building that was also renamed The Grand Hyatt New York.

In partnership with Hyatt, Trump covered the building in chrome and green glass, negotiated a 40-year, $60 million tax abatement agreement with New York City and reopened the project just as the New York real estate market was beginning to climb out of recession.

Trump gained more than a considerable financial reward for his solid efforts; he earned confidence in himself as a master negotiator. As George Ross explained:

"Trump pulled it off, convincing all these parties to work with him, using his enthusiasm, relationship-building skills, showmanship, preparation, and tenacity."

Trump's banker for The Grand Hyatt New York, Equitable Life, also began to see confidence in the young developer's vision and that would spark a new relationship in which the borrower and lender would align with other well-known projects such as Trump Tower (Chapter 2).

By 1987, gross operating profits at the Hyatt exceeded $30 million per year and in 1996 – around 15 years after opening – Trump sold his interest in the property to Hyatt Corporation for a whopping $142 million.

When Trump started, he had very little "skin in the game." He had structured the Grand Hyatt deal in a partnership with Hyatt (and the Pritzker family) and obtained the majority of funding from Equitable, establishing himself as a big league developer who could deliver a quality project on budget and on-time.

Most importantly, he had proven to himself that he could create large sums of wealth by converting a mental blueprint into an irreplaceable work of art. The Grand Hyatt would serve as a vision and catalyst for Trump to launch his own chain of hotels around the globe.

Who would have known that when Trump was developing his first high-end hotel in 1980 he would one day become New York's designer-label developer?

After conquering The Grand Hyatt, Trump was moving down the street along 5th Avenue to Park Place, the corresponding Monopoly property to that of Trump Tower.

It didn't take him long to get back into the hotel business. In 1988, he purchased the Plaza Hotel for $407.5 million. The iconic French Renaissance château-style building was designed by Henry Janeway Hardenbergh and opened to the public on October 1, 1907. At the time, it cost $12.5 million to construct. When the hotel opened, a room at the Plaza Hotel was only $2.50 per night, the equivalent of $63 today.

However, four years after Trump purchased The Plaza, he handed the keys back to the lender in a prepackaged bankruptcy (as discussed in Chapter 1). The lessons that Trump learned while building the Grand Hyatt and The Plaza would serve as constant reminders that real estate can be very rewarding, but leverage can be extremely risky.

While looking out of Trump's corner office – the Tiffany Corner – the billionaire investor can view The Plaza below. I am certain that it serves as a humbling reminder that high leverage can cripple profits. Trump acquired the Plaza for $407.5 million and spent over $50 million on renovations. His lead bank, Citibank, later forced him to take a 49 percent stake in the hotel in exchange for forgiving $250 million in debt.

But by the time Trump had turned 41, he had already owned and managed two of the best-known hotels in the world – one which made millions and the other which eventually cost the banks millions. Trump never lost money personally on The Plaza, and it was actually profitable when he owned it.

However, Trump learned more from the two hotel deals than he could have learned in any class at Wharton. He knew he was capable of scaling his successes by learning from his failures and had found the secret formula to make him richer than he ever imagined by leveraging his brand.

When Trump acquired The Plaza, he was over-leveraged. The concept of owning Boardwalk without passing GO seemed too good to be true. Then Trump landed on a corporate bankruptcy card and learned to become a more risk-averse investor.

Over the years, The Plaza and Trump's casinos and hotels in Atlantic City would serve as a constant reminder that bigger was not always better. The rush to wealth creation using highly-leveraged debt became the billionaire's well-known vice. While many wealthy investors form an addiction to drugs, alcohol, or sex, Trump's intoxication was getting rich quickly.

All of us are human, and while Donald Trump has an aura of invincibility, it's indisputable that the 70-year-old real estate investor went through tough financial times. As the legendary investor Benjamin Graham reminds us, *"Adversity is bitter sweet."*

Even after watching the Trump Empire crumbling before his eyes, Trump always maintained confidence that he could win. He had witnessed success early in life and he knew that if he could make over $140 million on The Grand Hyatt with less than $1 million of his money, he could do it again, and this time he would be much wiser.

Trump spent the next few years building residential towers in New York City and it was not until 1996 that he decided to take his next giant step. He began projects on Columbus Circle and the West Side rail yards helping to transform the West Side of Manhattan and virtually inventing the high-end condominium business on his own in New York.

The skyscraper, formerly known as the Gulf and Western Building, was remade in 1996 and Trump renamed it the Trump International Hotel and Tower. General Electric put up the money to transform the building and even though Trump invested a small sum, around $11 million, he was able to plaster his name across the building in 4-foot letters on the white-marble tower, always focusing on the brand.

The Trump International Hotel and Tower opened in 1996, just a few years after Trump parted with his nearby work of art, The Plaza Hotel, self-described as his "Mona Lisa." Trump must have intended to make a statement when the brand new 52-story gold-tinted hotel opened for business only several blocks away on Central Park South. He had transformed the structure into what *The New York Times* called:

"...Fancier than Trump Tower. Glitzier than Trump Taj Mahal. Pricier than Trump Palace or Trump Park."

The new Trump property contained 166 condominiums and 168 hotel suites featuring nine-foot windows, 10-foot ceilings, and sprawling space (up to 5,500 square feet). The new hotel was important for Trump because he could show the world that he had been down, but he was not out. *The New York Times* wrote:

"Even Mr. Trump's habitual critics seem willing to concede his comeback, if only because they have missed making fun of him."

The stamp of "irreplaceability" was evident and *The New York Times* reporter explained:

"Without such quintessentially Trump touches – brown reflective glass, stainless steel strips – the developer said his new tower would be just another building."

In over two decades, Trump International Hotel and Tower has become a highly profitable enterprise and much of that success is due to Trump's well-known skill set of being a promoter. He once said:

"I don't think I'm a good promoter. I think I really know how to build something that is beautiful, and it promotes itself."

The Brand Was Established

Trump was a little-known developer when he began his first big deal – converting the Commodore Hotel into the Grand Hyatt – but when Trump Tower opened, followed by The Trump International Hotel and Tower, he was a relevant developer known for excellence.

After that roaring success, it was clear that the billionaire had become a more conservative investor. He knew that the best way for him to grow his net worth was to utilize the cheapest form of currency – other people's money (or OPM).

OPM is what Trump would refer to as his real estate licensing business once acknowledging he could leverage his name in exchange for multiple sources of income. For example, Trump would take in fees for condo sales at the Trump International Hotel and Tower and then his management company could collect on-going revenue for managing the condo and hotel operations. Essentially, this means that Trump gets multiple bites of the apple – he collects licensing fees, development fees, marketing fees, and management fees.

This structure was less common in New York City at the time and Trump knew that he could exploit the business and begin to expand into other markets. In addition to sales and management fees, Trump began to grow his hotel business using OPM. He decided to seek out high-quality locations with experienced development partners. When a suitable site was located, Trump would charge the developer a licensing fee - averaging 10 percent - as well as construction management fees - averaging 10 percent.

By enforcing strict control over the design, construction, and leasing-up process, Trump forged a model that could provide scale and increased brand recognition across the globe. Trump began to roll out similar combined hotel and condominium projects in Las Vegas (Chapter 7) and Chicago (Chapter 6), and in 2010 he opened another hotel in New York.

The Trump SoHo was announced in 2006 and it officially opened in 2010, just as the recession ended. The 46-story tower, located at Varick Street and Sixth Avenue, was a collaboration between Trump, the Bayrock Group, and Tamir Sapir. This was one of the first hotel deals in which Trump used OPM without investing a dime of his own capital.

Trump then opened a 462-room luxury hotel in Waikiki in 2010, followed by a 70-story tower in Panama in 2011 – both licensing deals. In 2012, Trump planted a flag in Toronto with the 65-story tower that overlooks downtown Toronto's financial and entertainment district. Trump has another licensing project set to open in Vancouver in 2016 and projects have been announced for Rio and Bali.

In total, Trump has 15 owned and/or licensed hotels, either open or in the pipeline, and the company plans to own 20 hotels by 2020. The next opening is in Washington, DC where Trump is underway on a world-class hotel located along Pennsylvania Avenue (Chapter 8).

There's a tremendous opportunity for Trump to scale his hotel collection by extending his brand into domestic and international markets. In the U.S., Trump intends to open hotels in nearly all major gateway markets such as San Francisco, Los Angeles, Portland, Dallas, Houston, Atlanta, Boston, Philadelphia, and Phoenix.

Internationally, Trump has just begun to scratch the surface and has recently opened an office in China to explore opportunities for growing the Trump brand in Asia. One benefit for Trump is that he can also cross-market many of his hotels with his golf courses providing synergies in which a golf member at a Trump club could get discounts at Trump hotels and vise-versa.

Trump has multiple golf properties in Florida so a golf member could gain priority access to Trump's area lodging properties. Likewise, Trump owns and/or manages several courses within an hour's drive of New York City and golf members could benefit from having lodging privileges in New York City.

As Trump begins to gain scale - 20 hotels by 2020 - he will begin to extrapolate better terms with vendors so he can squeeze out better profit margins. Also, Trump has invested in a digital marketing platform to keep guests and prospective guests aware of specials and maintain awareness of the Trump brand.

Because Trump's company is private, it's harder to determine the value of the hotel licensing business. The fees that are generated are not as predictable as rent checks and are often lumpy or inconsistent due to the characteristically volatile construction and development process.

However, the non-owned hotel business is a substantial part of the Trump empire and should be included in the overall valuation of the billionaire. The income that is generated from the 15 operating hotels is considerable and we believe that Trump could easily ramp up the expansion of the hotel licensing business by adding at least two new hotels per year over the next decade.

This means that Trump could have forty owned and/or licensed hotels by 2030. Given the more recent exposure with Trump as a result of the presidential campaign, this forecast appears likely and could generate significant equity for Trump, his children, and insiders.

To model the hotel licensing business, we looked at the average costs to build all of the Trump-branded hotels and we arrived at a development cost of $500 million per property. Then we determined that Trump generates development and construction management fees of 5 percent per building. We continued by modeling the residential sales at 5 percent each over a course of ten years and added recurring management fees of 5 percent based on our forecasted revenue.

Assuming Trump rolls out two new projects per year, we forecast that Trump's licensing business could generate around $55 million annually as the company expands into new markets. Additionally, Trump gains an even more predictable revenue stream in which the company can manage the operations for the third-party owners.

We suspect that Trump is now receiving hotel management income of between $30 million to $50 million, and if the company opens 15 more properties before 2030, the fee income could top $75 million annually.

Obviously, 30 Trump hotels by 2030 is a forecast so it's not fair to value the future pipeline. In order to arrive at the value of the hotel licensing business, we opted to utilize mid-point recurring revenue projections of $37.5 million and the forecasted growth of two hotels per year. Our pro forma income for Trump's hotel licensing is $92 million in gross income.

We have estimated general and administrative (G&A) costs to be 12 percent and that translates into a forecasted annualized net income of $81 million. Since this is fee income, not owned real estate, we are using a 10 percent multiple which values the Trump hotel licensing business at $810 million.

The Trump-owned hotel assets are included in other chapters; however, Trump does have residual income from the Trump International Hotel and Tower in New York. Trump owns several units there as well as the space leased to the world-famous restaurant run by Jean-Georges Vongerichten – whom Trump has proclaimed *"the best chef in New York."*

Fred Trump would have never conceived of one of his grandchildren becoming a legend in the hotel sector. In addition to the fact that the two share the same last name, both ambitious investors sought to become a relevant force by focusing on Luxury, luxury, and luxury.

Other common attributes for the two include hard work, discipline, and a refusal to fail. Jan A. deRoos, Ph.D., HVS Professor of Hotel Finance and Real Estate at Cornell University explains:

"The Trump Hotel Collection is one of the world's few true luxury hotel brands. While it competes with the likes of Four Seasons, Jumeirah, and Shangri La, the Trump hotel brand offers a unique value proposition to hotel owners seeking an alternative. The brand is synonymous with the extravagance, opulence, and lavishness that has always been associated with the Trump personality. While the Trump brand is often associated with golf oriented properties, all Trump Hotels, whether affiliated with a golf course or not, have a set of facilities and amenities that are expected in a luxury hotel. What Trump does so well is take what is expected and to deliver these 'expectations' in truly unique and interesting ways. The suites are over the top, the meeting spaces sparkle in ways that are not found anywhere else in the world, the restaurant has a Michelin ranked chef with a truly special wine list, the staff are disciplined professionals oriented to the highest levels of service and the hotel is designed to be connected to its urban or resort environment in a natural way."

Donald Trump was close to financial ruin, but he was able to transform himself into a greater investor by leveraging his name and not his savings. The Trump Hotel business has become a significant business line for The Trump Organization and Donald Trump has created the ultimate "sleep well at night" platform – generating reliable and predictable profits using other people's money. In the last chapter of the book, we will provide more secrets on how Donald Trump has built his million-dollar branding empire.

CHAPTER 6

TRUMP INTERNATIONAL HOTEL AND TOWER CHICAGO

"As long as you're going to be thinking anyway, think big."
– Donald Trump

Bill Rancic, the winner of "The Apprentice" during its first season, selected the job overseeing construction of this handsome project in Chicago over a senior management role at Trump's Los Angeles National Golf Course Resort. Apparently, the opportunity to become involved in a massive new mixed-use, class A construction project was more appealing than warm weather.

The elegantly designed Trump International Hotel and Tower in Chicago, Illinois opened on January 30, 2009, to rave reviews for both the hotel and residential components. The building's floor count and architectural height gave it the title of fourth tallest residential apartment or condominium, in the world.

The views from the building's upper floors are spectacular. The property is situated on the bank of the Chicago River with views of the entry to Lake Michigan beyond. A series of bridges that span the Chicago River are visible from the building and provide a magical view at night.

The sheer size of the building is a massive 2.6 million square feet. Designed by Skidmore, Owings & Merrill, Trump International Hotel and Tower is wrapped in a polished stainless steel with an anodized aluminum façade treatment that glimmers in the Chicago sun.

The exterior structure includes a powerful layered design as the building rises. This design, along with rounded edges of the exterior, helps ameliorate drag effects which can occur in Chicago due to high winds.

Drag, precipitated by the wind, can apply severe pressure to any architectural obstacle such as flat panels or edges during periods of high-speed gusts and snap elements off their base. Since opening in 2009, there have been no reports of wind damage to the skyscraper.

The tower is home to 486 luxury condominium units and 339 hotel rooms making it a large mixed-use property. A 1.2-acre riverfront park is adjacent to the building and provides a softer curb appeal to the massive property.

Some Controversy

Trump's imposing structure came with its own controversy. One particular issue stemmed from the park. The landscaping received special recognition from Mayor Daley's *Landscape Awards*. The press release announced the award to "Trump Park" and touted the generous use of sumac trees, ferns, and other indigenous plantings in a *"poetic interpretation of native Illinois... at once sophisticated and familiar."*

The following year, the award winning landscaping was completely ripped out and replaced by a set of evergreens requiring much less watering and care. Then the trees were lit in the evenings conflicting with the city's objective of a "dark night sky" to facilitate better stargazing.

Another controversy arose during the pre-sale effort for the condominium residences. Trump provided a "friends and family" set of benefits for early pre-sales and provided the sales department a list of people who qualified for special pricing along with a smaller down payment. As sales began to take off and the prices rose, Trump eliminated the "friends and family" package of benefits.

This angered many purchasers who were on the list and planned to buy a condominium in the building. The initial selling price of the condominiums was set at $500 per square foot. Demand escalated and the prices rose to a high of $1300 per square foot. Several of those purchasers who planned to buy units at the lower price were caught in the cancellation of their benefits package and sued Trump.

Present Day

Now in its seventh year, the project has been a huge success. The hotel reports strong occupancy and average daily rates (ADR) and the condominiums have been sold out for years.

We visited the 5-Star hotel and condominium in late 2014 and were amazed at the attention to detail. Trump certainly knows how to win over customers. In December 2014, he closed a deal to purchase the top floor with Sanjay Shah, the founder and CEO of Vistex.

We toured the penthouse that Shah purchased. The 14,260 square-foot unit was unfinished at the time with only the drywall and concrete floors completed. The circular unit has stunning 360-degree views allowing Trump to collect $17 million in cash for the 89th-floor penthouse.

Trump was asking $32 million and, even though Trump settled for less than the sticker price, the purchase by Shah eclipsed billionaire Ken Griffin's 2012 purchase of a condo on the 66th floor of the Park Tower for $15 million. Shah explained:

"I've traveled all around the world, but just in terms of the architecture, even if you go to New York, there are other high-rises, but nothing quite as exotic as this. You can view every single landmark the city has. I think that's what appealed to me most about it."

Several other units have since traded for near record prices due in large part to the luxury of the property along with the unparalleled views from the upper floors. The lower floors also enjoy a significant amount of light pouring into the residences and hotel rooms. The common areas are elegantly designed and the property is reported to be extremely well maintained. No notable complaints have been registered about any aspect of the property. This is a major win given the scale of this project.

While Trump certainly had hoped that prices would rise, we doubt that he had any idea how quickly demand would increase to justify the extent of the rising prices. This is a rare occasion when Donald Trump didn't anticipate the degree of free market success. In other cases, he has priced condominiums at the very high end of the market only to face slow sales, discounting prices or giving some sort of concession to stimulate them. Not in Chicago.

The combination of a well-received building design, the fabulous interior common areas, the views from the condominiums, and the combination of modern amenities such as the on-site health club, the party room, the large parking garage, and the fine park adjacent to the property, all helped elevate the value of the project.

A Historical Perspective

In 2001, prior to the 9/11 terrorist attacks on the United States, Donald Trump had announced plans for the new Chicago skyscraper. The original plan was for it to be the tallest building in the world. The combination of enormously strong bedrock at the site, the cacophony of skyscrapers dotting the Chicago skyline, and the overall acceptance level for high-rises by the people of Chicago, provided the essential elements to make a go of it.

And of course, Donald Trump's vision to continue to push the boundaries of real estate development science was a major factor. In meeting after meeting with premier architects and engineers, all collaborating on what just might be a record-breaking, first-class mixed-use tower, the mood was electric. This could be the perfect blend of location, developer, and usage.

Many people don't give Donald Trump enough credit for seeing the future of real estate as a "live, work, play" combination. He went forward with his blueprint without relying on studies to ultimately prove his point.

Those developers who waited until various research reports were written underscoring the popularity of "live, work, play" real estate projects were cautious in their approach and needed "confirmation" that it works.

Donald Trump did not need third-party confirmation to recognize that he too liked living in the same building where he worked. He can shop, dine, work, and live within steps of each aspect of his life. Who wouldn't enjoy that convenience?

Once the 9/11 attacks hit, Donald Trump scaled back the ambitious plans to build the world's tallest building in Chicago. This decision isn't well known to many; yet it reflects his real sense of understanding when to take very bold steps and when to hold back. The building was redrawn to a lower height threshold and still maintains a record-setting height for a residential tower.

A Trophy Valuation

A common element found throughout the portfolio of development projects built by Donald Trump is the ultra-luxurious nature of each property. No detail is overlooked and every single decision is predicated on the creation of the finest asset possible.

There are many iconic projects that share this common thread but rarely do these properties come on the market. When they do, a bidding war breaks out, and when the proverbial dust settles, the final potential purchasers are usually foreign buyers who want to move capital from their country to the United States.

The "cap rate," or "yield on cost," or even the internal rate of return metrics, don't drive the process paid for true trophy assets. Rather, it is their rarity and ability to retain the value that draws investors. These purchasers do not generally finance their acquisitions with debt. They are attempting to relocate as much capital as possible from a home country that may have blistering inflation, a wilting currency exchange ratio to the US dollar, and may also be involved in both domestic and international conflicts.

Regardless of the specific purpose, the United States and, in particular, the high quality real estate here represents a true "safe haven" for billions, if not trillions of dollars for these investors.

In a recent highly publicized case, Anbang Insurance Company, a China-based investor, sought to acquire Starwood International, the worldwide lodging company. The price for Starwood ultimately reached over $13 billion and it was Marriott International who won the rights to acquire Starwood.

Meanwhile, Anbang made several competitive offers, only to be told by Chinese insurance regulators that the company would exceed its annual overseas investment threshold. Prior to bidding on Starwood, Anbang acquired the famous Waldorf-Astoria hotel located at 300 Park Avenue in New York City for $1.95 billion. Anbang has invested heavily outside of China, home to the company, which has surprisingly been in business for barely over a decade.

The point in this soliloquy is that assets like Trump International Hotel and Tower, the few that exist, should be valued through a different lens than a traditional class A property.

Our Valuation Method

First and foremost, the sales of the building's 486 condominium units greatly reduced the overall basis for the property. The lowest price of the condominiums was set at $500 per square foot for "friends and family" purchasers. This technique was both ceremonial and economic.

Trump wanted to spur early buyers to show a high level of acceptance of the project before completion. He didn't realize how successful it would become as prices rose to a level of $1300 per square foot. As mentioned above, he canceled the friends and family discount, angering many prospective buyers.

Condos:	486 59%	1.534 thousand square feet (MSF)
Hotel rooms:	339 41%	1.066 (MSF)
Total:	825 100%	2.600 (MSF)
Total Development Cost (TDC):		$847million (mm)
Condominium Allocation:		$500(mm)

Remember, the TDC *includes* not only the condominiums and hotel rooms but the *entirety* of the project itself. Food and beverage sales, parking lot income, event charges, and much more emanate from the 2.6 million square feet of the project. This calculation will be performed in easy-to-understand logical math, but will be very conservative to be fair.

Using the 1.534 million square feet allocation to the condominiums and an average valuation of $1,000 per square foot, we achieve condo sell-out proceeds at $1.534 billion, or nearly twice the entire development cost. We will reduce the size of the allocation by a full 20 percent to set aside for common areas and other uses and will do the same for the hotel, next.

This leaves us with 1,227,200 square feet at $1,000 per square foot or $1,227,200,000 in condo sales. The condominium sales should provide enough proceeds to cover the cost of development by almost double the amount.

Based upon 2015 comparable sales for high-quality trophy hotels across the United States, we arrive at metrics that range from $750k per room key to $1.2mm per room key.

To evaluate the value for Trump's Chicago hotel we decided it was important to consider whether or not the property was union or non-union. A non-union property means that it is less profitable. Also, we considered the hotel's amenities and location. All of these metrics scored well and thus we opted to use $1,000 per key – the high-end of the range considering Chicago is a slightly overbuilt market.

The hotel contains 339 hotel rooms that can be valued, nominally, at $339 million using the mid-end range for trophy hotels. This is a gross sales number and includes the benefits of all other service fee income.

Regardless of the developer's basis in the asset, the hotel itself has tremendous implicit value. It is obvious that the project was a financial success, however, the financial engineering structured to absorb all of the development and operating costs must also be addressed.

We suspect that a large portion of the residential proceeds for The Chicago Tower was used to pay down the original $640 million construction loan. In fact, based on our analysis, it appears that Trump could have already paid off the loan nearly two times with estimated gross sales profits of $1.2 billion.

Our records indicate there is still secured debt on the property and the Federal Election Campaign (FEC) filings indicate a loan balance in excess of $50 million. To err on the safe side, we will assume leverage of $75 million, and that translates into net equity of $264 million.

It's important to recognize that this is an equity valuation because Trump has low leverage on the building and substantial cash flow being generated. For modeling purposes, we have assumed that Trump has moved around $300 million of the sales proceeds over to cash and marketable securities (assuming his tax bracket is 39.6 percent in 2016, we subtracted approximately $200 million for Uncle Sam and divided the rest between his two liquid asset categories – cash and marketable securities).

Trump International Hotel and Tower Chicago is a trophy asset and it's important to recognize that this "cash cow" has generated immense wealth for the billionaire. By selling off the residential units, Trump was able to maintain conservative leverage and generate steady and reliable income from his remaining hotel units.

In addition to profits generated from development and sales (discussed in Chapter 5), Trump will continue to see dividends from his hotel (estimated at $100 million per year). Most importantly, Trump has planted a flag in one America's largest gateway markets validating that the model is working and the pipeline can easily be extended into other influential markets such as Atlanta, Dallas, San Francisco, Los Angeles, Boston, and Portland.

The Trump Factor

TRUMP INTL. CHICAGO				
Properties	Units	Sq. Ft.	$/Sq. Ft.	Totals
Residential Units	486	1,227,200	$1,000	$1,227,200,000
Hotel Units	339	na	1,000	339,000,000
Total				888,200,000
Construction Loan				640,000,000
Debt				(75,000,000)
Trump Equity				$264,000,000

CHAPTER 7

TRUMP INTERNATIONAL LAS VEGAS

"When I hear 'recession,' I ask,
'What have you got for sale?'"
– Phil Ruffin

Although Donald Trump's 64-story luxury hotel, condominium, and timeshare in Las Vegas are game-free, the billionaire investor is no stranger to gaming (as discussed in Chapter 1), having rolled the dice in a big bet Atlantic City.

When Trump and his Las Vegas partners, Phil Ruffin, and Jack Wishna, decided to construct a tower on 3.46 acres near the Fashion Show Mall (owned by GGP), the gaming market was on fire. The project was designed in two phases, with Tower 1 being constructed first and Tower 2 to come later, possibly to include gambling.

Trump and his partners locked in construction costs on the Trump International before breaking ground in 2005, but it took around three years before the first shovel went in the ground. The project was first announced by Ruffin in April 2002 and it was initially going to consist of a 60-story tower with an expected cost of around $300 million.

However, in August 2003 Ruffin revised the plan to 43-stories at a cost of $272 million.

In November 2003, the building boom had commenced in Las Vegas and Trump and Ruffin had to make up some time on the $2 billion Wynn Las Vegas that was set to open in 2005. Although Trump had never competed directly with billionaire, Steve Wynn, in Las Vegas, many were aware of the showmanship, as Trump said:

"Steve (Wynn) is building right across the street, and with Fashion Show, we think the site is terrific."

Trump said that he was considering "something on a larger scale" for the project and in July 2004, the partners decided to scrap the smaller concept and replace it with a larger one – a 645-foot tower at a cost of around $300 million. The 3.46 acre site was developed on a vacant parcel of land directly across from the Nordstrom and Robinson-May department stores at the Fashion Show Mall.

Although The Wynn was under construction in 2005, there was very little new construction near the Trump hotel site. However, in 2003 a major expansion of the Fashion Show Mall was completed. Two-hundred thousand square feet of retail space was built extending out of the backside of the mall between Robinsons-May and Macy's.

At two million square feet, Fashion Show Mall is the largest shopping destination on the Las Vegas Strip and one of the largest shopping centers in the USA.

Dillard's and Saks Fifth Avenue moved to a new, larger locations in this new wing, alongside a Bloomingdale's Home store and Nordstrom. Neiman Marcus, Macy's, and Robinsons-May expanded their stores; the former Saks Fifth Avenue was razed and replaced by several restaurants, a food court, and a strip-facing plaza called "The Cloud."

In September 2006, following Federated's purchase of May Department Stores, Robinsons-May was converted to a second Macy's store. The store was shuttered in 2008 and remained empty until 2013 when it was converted into a wing of shops and a separate Macy's Men store.

Just as the Great Recession was unfolding, Trump and Ruffin's Tower 1 opened on March 31, 2008. This had to be the absolute worst time to open a hotel project in Las Vegas. The rooms were not renting and the condominium market was also hit hard with many prospective owners unable to close on their units creating a double-whammy for Trump and Ruffin.

A Combination of Experience and Relationships

The good thing for Trump was that he had already been down that road before (see Chapter 1) and his partner, Ruffin, was equally battle-tested.

Unlike Trump, Ruffin was not college educated and, at his current age of 80, is the product of the "school of hard knocks" beginning when he parlayed his first deal – he bought a gas station in Kansas – into an enormous collection of real estate properties, ranging from shopping centers, office parks, and hotels.

Around the same time that Trump and Ruffin were opening their Las Vegas Tower, Ruffin was closing on another tower just on the other side of The Fashion Show Mall. MGM owned Treasure Island, worth around $1.3 billion in 2009, and Ruffin was able to wrestle the resort away from Carl Icahn (approximate net worth of $10 billion according to *Forbes* at that time) for around half of that amount, or $755 million.

Ruffin was one of the few Las Vegas insiders with the cash to make such a deal, but he also had experience at flipping big deals for a profit. In 1998, he bought the Vegas Strip's New Frontier Hotel & Casino for $165 million and then sold it to Israeli billionaire Yitzhak Tshuva (the net worth soaring to $4.5 billion by 2014 according to *Forbes*) for $1.2 billion.

Trump not only teamed up with a partner with deep pockets, but Ruffin is the one local player in Las Vegas who knows the poker business in and out. He once beat out five other billionaires, including Ron Burkle, at a charity poker game.

It appears that Trump and Ruffin are long-time friends. However, unlike Trump, Ruffin maintains a low profile, but in addition to his billionaire elite status (worth roughly $ 2.4 billion according to *Forbes*), the two share a taste in marrying models. Ruffin married the 2004 Miss Ukraine winner, Oleksandra Nikolayenko, in 2008 and Trump was the best man at the wedding.

Ruffin is an intensely private person who plays his cards very close to his chest—poker is his game, after all—when it comes to talking about his kids and second wife, former Miss Ukraine Oleksandra Nikolayenko, he is an open book.

"I would recommend starting a second family to anybody—it's really worth it," he says. "You have to kind of relive everything."

Adversity Leads to Solutions

Ruffin and Trump had another thing in common (in addition to having five kids and beautiful spouses), the two billionaires have experienced adversity. Because they were experienced at making mistakes, they were better equipped to wrestle with the challenges of the Great Recession.

The Las Vegas Sun wrote:

"While others grew their fortunes with Wall Street money, Ruffin was offering $1.99 margaritas and bikini bull riding at the New Frontier."

Trump and Ruffin, both cutthroat businessmen, had been trained in the school of hard knocks and their more recent conservative habits would pay off.

In 2009, the 64-story, casino-free building, wrapped in 24-karat, gold-infused glass was standing out like a sore thumb. Several other towers had started nearby but the work had halted as lenders and investors were scrambling to cut losses. Silent cranes were hovering above the steel and concrete skeleton of the adjacent Echelon project.

Once a symbol of prosperity, the Echelon project was conceived as a cutting edge luxury mega-resort on the Strip's north end. Also, nearby was the Las Vegas Plaza and Fontainebleau Las Vegas, a hulking bluish-green tower that was 70 percent finished when construction halted.

In what was arguable the darkest days of the recession, Trump Hotel Las Vegas officially opened in March of 2008, and a grand opening ceremony was held by Trump and Ruffin on April 11, 2008. The final cost of the project was approximately $500 million. The building had 1,282 units – a combination of hotel rooms and condominiums.

By October 2008, Las Vegas was a ghost town; only 21 percent of condo unit sales had closed as potential buyers had trouble securing mortgages. Several investors sued Trump and Ruffin alleging that they were defrauded by Trump's sales team. Investors claimed that the sales representatives promised high-yield returns on units that they argued could fetch as much as $600 per night as part of the property's rental pool.

Trump and Ruffin changed strategy, opting to lease out the condos, listing all of the units for lease, including studios, one bedrooms, two bedrooms, and penthouses. This seemed like a logical option for the two to generate more operating revenue while also reducing operating costs for the hotel.

The hotel units, offered for longer periods, are attractive to companies that bring in accountants and other executives doing temporary work and needing a place for three months or longer. Even high-rollers who travel to Vegas might not want to buy in Las Vegas, but desire a furnished place they can live in short-term.

In September 2012, the Trump Organization announced that it sold roughly 300 condominium units in Trump International Hotel Las Vegas to Hilton Worldwide's timeshare division, Hilton Grand Vacations, this was especially satisfying for Trump and Ruffin to reduce their debt exposure. In late 2015, Ruffin said:

"... the building is almost all paid for. He (Trump) made $100 million on the timeshare deal. We started out with $567 million in debt that's now down to $12 million. We still have 400 units left to sell."

Trump's units were initially priced to start at $600,000 and ascend to $6 million. When I stayed at Trump Las Vegas I was told that a studio could be had for about $250,000. Scanning area comparable sales for Trump Vegas units ranging from 441 square feet to 533 square feet, I found them selling for around $565 per square foot. There are a few larger suites available – one 1,529 square foot unit – selling for $1.1 million ($719 per square foot).

The Assessment

We spoke with a local appraiser and he said that $565 per square foot would be the retail value of each unit and *"from a current value perspective (the) bulk value assuming a sale to a single purchaser would be considerably less."* As he explained, you would need to take into account costs associated with the sell-out, referring to sales commissions, closing costs, marketing expenses and the like. He said, a *"discount of 20 to 30 percent would be required."*

There is a high demand for Trump units in Las Vegas as high-rise condo units have begun to increase in value since the financial crash. According to Howard Klein, a former V.P. at Taj Mahal, supply is in check now:

> *"MGM's latest earnings release outlook signals no significant expansion. The Vegas market should not see many new deals after Genting."*

Klein is referring to the massive casino nearing completion adjacent to Trump's site. Sandwiched between the new 3,000 room, 56-story Resorts World (expected to open in 2018) and the recently renovated Fashion Mall, Trump Las Vegas will benefit considerably in years to come.

Trump is more in favor of holding his winners as Klein suggests, *"He likes to doggedly hold onto assets."* (Klein told us he used to work for Donald Trump)

Donald Trump's son, Eric Trump, oversees operations at the casino-free tower. In what was once a speculative project on a less-glamorous end of The Strip, there is now a flurry of activity around the site including the brand new casino and adjacent hotel. The patience has paid off for Trump and Ruffin and this property is now generating substantial cash flow, even though there are no slot machines in the building.

Sources indicate that a second tower may be in the works on a parcel that Ruffin owns alongside the tower. The proposed site is currently a hotel parking lot and the new deal would include a casino. Ruffin said the casino would be connected to the existing hotel and that he is now contemplating a $100 million casino with Trump as a 50 percent partner. Who knows, maybe Donald Trump will try another roll of the dice. If so, I'm sure it will be with much less leverage than Atlantic City and with another billionaire backing him.

Trump manages the Las Vegas property and we have already included that revenue stream in the previous chapter. The hotel excluding debt is worth around $113 million (400 units at around $282,000 per unit).

This valuation is conservative since we did not include any of the most expensive units. However, we did include around $4 million in value related to units that Trump owns personally. After deducting bulk selling costs and the current debt ($12 million), we value Trump's fifty percent interest in the Las Vegas property at $48.5 million.

We also made reference to the $100 million in cash generated from the bulk sale to Hilton that will appear on the liquid asset portion of the balance sheet discussed in Chapter 15.

While many high-rolling developers went broke in the last recession, Trump and Ruffin were able to survive and ride out the devastating financial tsunami. It was because of Trump's more risk-averse mindset that he opted to partner with a rich businessman who had experience as the local sharpshooter.

The discipline paid off and the duo maintained patience that was ultimately rewarded and continues to produce stable and predictable cash flow without the volatility of the more speculative gaming operations.

I once heard a friend say that *"When you lay down with dogs you end up with fleas."* However, that is certainly not the case as it relates to Trump and Ruffin. The duo has much more in common than being wealth billionaires; they are also disciplined investors. They have considerable combined investment experiences and, as the legendary investor, Ben Graham once said, *"The most durable education is self-education."*

The Trump Factor

TRUMP INTL. LAS VEGAS

Properties	Units	Av. Sq. Ft.	$/Sq. Ft.	Totals
Trump-owned				$4,000,000
Hotel Units	400	500	$565	113,000,000
Total				117,000,000
Bulk Discount			10%	(11,300,000)
Loan Balance				(12,000,000)
Trump Equity			50%	$48,850,000

CHAPTER 8

TRUMP INTERNATIONAL HOTEL WASHINGTON DC

"The two most important requirements for major success are: first, being in the right place at the right time, and second, doing something about it."
– Ray Kroc

In 2014, Donald Trump's organization won the rights to lease the Old Post Office Pavilion located on Pennsylvania Avenue NW, in downtown Washington, D.C. for a period of 99 years. He is forging ahead with construction now to convert this beautiful old building into a first-class luxury hotel that should be open in September 2016.

Trump will face formidable competition in the luxury hotel market in Washington, D.C. However, like all things Trump, he will move heaven and earth to ensure its success. This is a look at the property, the game plan, and the competition it will face once it is completed.

Location, Location, Location

The property is located directly on Pennsylvania Avenue and was originally built in 1892 in the Romanesque Revival style. Willoughby J. Edbrooke was the architect of record for the original structure. In addition, designed by Karn Charuhas Chapman & Twohey, the East Atrium was added in 1899 in a Modernist style. The entire property is listed on the National Register of Historic Places.

Located at 11th Street and Pennsylvania Avenue, it stands at the virtual midpoint between the White House and the U.S. Capitol Building on a promenade that is the most famous street in America, if not the world. Government agencies, international organizations, courthouses, and a flurry of restaurants surround the property.

At this location in Washington, the streets are wide, the sidewalks enormous, and the infrastructure designed to handle the masses of people who attend parades and activities along the avenue throughout the year. The Metrorail's Federal Triangle Metro stop is across the street from the site on 12th Street; otherwise, access is mainly by walking, public bus transportation, taxi and Uber, or private driver.

The only real pedestrian use is for tourists who want to take in the many museums and sites located on Constitution and Independence Avenues. The National Mall is located along two blocks due south of the building and is within walking distance. Once there, tourists can stroll east to the Capitol and west to the back lawn of the White House and over to the Washington Monument.

The physical structure itself is a handsome limestone property with a tall, imposing clock tower. It served for 15 years as the headquarters for the United States Postal Service until remanded back to the General Services Administration (GSA). The Post Office had grown so dramatically that it no longer fit into the space. It was used as offices for several U.S. Government agencies for decades thereafter.

Competition

Pennsylvania Avenue boasts a high concentration of luxury hotels providing direct competition to the proposed Trump International project. The closest hotels to the Trump project include:

The J.W. Marriott Hotel

Named for J. Willard Marriott himself, the founder of the company, this signature hotel is a prominent property on Pennsylvania and 15th Street, NW. The common areas include massive open spaces with nearly 100-foot ceilings. It is at the top of the Marriott food chain and the company is very proud of this line of hotels;

The Willard

This historic beaux-arts structure has endured many lives. It was finally acquired and renovated by The Oliver T. Carr Company in 1981 and reopened in 1986. It is now a pristine landmark located directly across 15th street to the west of the J.W. Marriott. The interior spaces of the hotel are confined, yet intimate. The exterior space gets most of its action on beautiful days. Tables for the outside café are popular and crowded weather permitting. The Willard is an elegant "old school" structure and is in need of rehabilitation again;

The W Hotel

For decades, this was The Hotel Washington. While it really isn't up to the standards of a luxury hotel, we will include it because of its location. Immediately adjacent to the Willard, its wide façade on 15th Street faces the Treasury Department next to The White House.

All three hotels mentioned thus far enjoy pedestrian access to the business district of Washington, D.C. The rooftop café and bar is a huge draw for the "W." Views from the rooftop deck are unparalleled and the National Mall, Pennsylvania Avenue, as well as the White House, can all be seen while you're sipping a gin and tonic and diving into a plate of salmon.

The Ritz-Carlton Georgetown

This is a tiny, but elegant hotel nestled in the streets of historic Georgetown. Its biggest asset is the ability of guests to walk out of the hotel and enjoy the activity and shops in the city of Georgetown which dates back to the 1700's. Like its cousin, it is a well-oiled operation and a favorite of those who enjoy boutique style luxury hotels.

Note: The Ritz-Carlton brand (and several hotels) was acquired by Marriott and now operated by the company. Both Georgetown and Washington, DC, located at the west end, have condominiums connected to them. The condos don't affect the operations of the hotels.

The Four Seasons

The granddaddy of Washington, DC. luxury hotels, it opened its doors in 1979, well ahead of any competitors. It instantly became "the hotel" to stay at when in the city. Neatly tucked into a site with a steep grade toward the Canal and the Parkway, the hotel's design features a huge entryway with two large entrance lanes for vehicles.

Bright lighting at the front door ensures maximum visibility for people entering the hotel. A silent aura surrounds visitors who whisper when entering the lobby as they walk toward the opulent Palm Court to the soft melody of a piano player. The Four Seasons defined "elegance" and continues to do so today.

The restaurant, Michael Mina's Bourbon Steak, occupies space on the lower level and continues the hushed elegance with deep wool carpeting and immediate table service upon entry. Airy, bright, and chic, the glass curtain wall at the south of the restaurant has inviting views of the historic Chesapeake and Ohio (C&O) canal and seasonal flowers and foliage. In the 1980s, *Desiree* opened and was the most popular disco in DC.

It closed to make way for the more modern member's only gym, another small luxury among the myriad of amenities justifiably boasted by the Ritz-Carlton.

Note: The physical exteriors of the above hotels are collectively simple. Bland is another word. All of these properties were originally constructed to be hotels and, therefore, focused their architectural attention on the interior spaces, not the exterior façade. Each has attempted to fit in with its immediate surroundings and succeeded. For example, both the Four Seasons and Ritz-Carlton Georgetown are built of red brick. The historic properties that surround the hotels are also of red brick, or painted over red brick, and the hotels blend in smoothly. The Willard is the only exception since it was developed during a period of more architectural flair – if there ever was one, in Washington, DC.

The St. Regis

This hotel is a conundrum. It is a key component to the storied St. Regis lineup (now owned by Starwood) and has many of the elegant components of its competitors. Yet, the location at 16th and K makes it more of a business-oriented hotel. Having only 182 rooms, it is on the small side.

The St. Regis Washington doesn't have a "King Cole Bar" or any famous watering hole like its NYC relative. The lobby has always been empty each time I have visited and I am curious and uncertain what the draw is for this hotel. There is no major exercise facility, no spa, or decent restaurant. Each time I have walked by, a letter or two is missing from the signage on K Street.

This simply gives me pause as to who is actually managing the details of the St. Regis Washington. Built in 1926, it gets points for an elegant façade, but the immediate surroundings don't excite anyone.

Mandarin Oriental, Washington

This hotel is a true outpost located in southwest Washington, DC, home to virtually 100 percent of the government agencies. The office buildings in this submarket all close up tightly at night and there is *zero* street activity. The driveway to the hotel is long and quiet.

Inside, the hotel is a busy place and has extraordinary common areas with massive ceiling heights and a very open feel. The glass curtain wall facing south to the Potomac River offers guests and visitors tremendous views.

Once you're inside, it is a cheery and luxurious place to stay. It has a spa, indoor pool, and large ballroom (10,800 square feet). With 400 guest rooms, this hotel is a formidable competitor to Trump. *Why?*

Because government agencies spawn a lot of private sector business and they want a very convenient location. It is the shortest distance to Ronald Reagan National Airport so you can easily make your flights. You will not face the DC traffic congestion, which has become notorious as new residents flood DC each year.

The Watergate Hotel

Soon to be back on the market, an international investor from France has acquired this well-known property. It is the Watergate office building that is well-known for scandal, but the hotel benefits from the infamous correlation since the name *Watergate* resonates with anyone age 45 and up.

The West End Hotels

Three luxury hotels sit on three of the four corners of 24th and M Streets NW and are considered to be in the heart of DC's west end. This location works well for visitors who want to be near, but not in Georgetown. The World Bank, IMF and International Finance Corporation are close by on Pennsylvania Avenue from 21st to 18th Streets.

The Fairmont Hotel

This elegant hotel has changed flags many times since its development in 1985. Vlastimil Koubek designed it in conjunction with the adjacent office buildings, both built by The Oliver T. Carr Company. With 415 rooms (including suites), it is a large hotel that incorporates a handsome lobby and sitting areas along with an outdoor area and pavilion for events. A busy circular driveway and porte-cochere on 24th street stay filled with limousines, taxis, and Uber drivers.

The Park Hyatt

This elegant Park Hyatt contains 216 guest rooms (including suites) and has a generous albeit bland lobby. Common areas include a unique "tea tasting room" with hundreds of blends of teas from the orient available. The *Blue Duck Tavern* is the hotel's restaurant made famous by First Lady Michelle Obama's hosting the President for a recent birthday party. It remains a favorite dining spot for the First Family. Designed by David Childs of Skidmore, Owings & Merrill LLP (SOM), it was built in 1986, one year after the Fairmont listed above.

The Westin Georgetown

Owned by Starwood Hotels, this attractive property contains 248 guest rooms and 25 suites. It was built in 1984 and developed by The Kaempfer Company along with the adjacent office building. This part of town has a unique zoning overlay called "HR" or Hotel/Residential. This requires a residential or hotel asset to be included when a new office building is planned. The Westin Georgetown is a bit of a misnomer as Georgetown is located several blocks to the west. Sited on the actual corner of 24th and M Streets, NW, the Westin is a very popular hotel especially for members of the Starwood Preferred Guest system (SPG).

The Ritz-Carlton Washington, D.C.

Located on 23rd between L and M Streets, this hotel is also located in the west end. It is a classic Ritz-Carlton with functionally elegant spaces. Everything works smoothly at this property, particularly service from the staff from the doormen to the valet, to the porters and others. Ritz-Carlton Washington is a precast neutral color stone, matching up nicely with the nearby understated office building environment.

Several restaurants are nearby; one is connected to the hotel. Meeting and ballrooms are large and appropriate for many organizations that require a large space and efficient operations. The memorial services for Jack Valenti, who reigned as the president of the Motion Picture Association of America, were held there.

Actors, producers, writers, and more from Hollywood descended on Washington to attend. Even with the record-breaking attendance by luminaries of the film industry, everything went like clockwork. Limousines were stationed around the hotel as far as the eye could see. Movie stars, Michael Douglas and his wife Catherine Zeta-Jones, were seen calmly waiting for their driver in the front porte-cochere – no one bothered them or sought autographs.

This is the guest profile Donald Trump wants to attract. President Obama, World Bank leaders and others have used the hotel frequently for events specifically for its reputation as a well-protected fortress.

Equinox, the well-known gym from New York City, recently acquired a massive, two-level gym that is part of the hotel. It encompasses 100,000 square feet and is an unparalleled exercise location with an indoor pool, the most advanced modern equipment, and its own large-scale café; and now . . . .

Trump International Hotel

This property is a true and rare *gem*. No other physical asset - hotel, office building, apartment building, or even museum in Washington, DC - has anything as elegant and grand as the architecture, street presence, and the *pure curb appeal* that the Old Post Office Pavilion boasts. It is simply a beautiful building and will likely be further enhanced with Trump's unique eye. Landscaping, lighting, and well-dressed valet, porters, and doormen will add to the cachet.

Trump's management team has informed us that there will be a curb cut on Pennsylvania Avenue to allow better-controlled access to the building near the front. The sidewalks in this area are massive. There may be another side of the property used for the "working reception" area to allow the front to be left as a postcard-worthy visage.

The current game plan is to set the entrance on 11th Street toward the western portion of the block where the addition stands. This is a very workable solution and maintains the pristine entryway in front from Pennsylvania Avenue.

Once inside, the full-height atrium is simply breathtaking and all sorts of venues will fill this area. Nothing was left to chance when this property was designed. From a purely physical perspective, it lends itself to a luxury hotel quite well. Sunlight splashes into all corners of the building from the massive atrium. Ironwork located on the floor to about the third level could never be replicated today. It's unique and expensive. It is unclear if there was a purpose for it other than decoration, but it certainly succeeds as a fascinating embellishment.

Everything is big; ceiling heights, walls, floors, walkways, and elevators are designed to be "grandiose." This property, once complete and operating, will be a city unto itself. While other luxury hotels may boast high ceilings, wide corridors, and common areas (like the J.W. Marriott), the Old Post Office Pavilion is in a singular class. The place is a colossal labyrinth and employees will surely be answering their guests' eternal question: "How do I get to . . . ?"

Impressive Amenities

Given the size and the location, the Trump International Hotel should strive to be a self-contained property with every conceivable amenity within the walls of the hotel. A luxurious spa, a high-tech gym with an indoor swimming pool, and exclusive hairdressers are basic requirements. Retail shops are essential to the experience and need to match the Trump brand and quality of others nearby.

Located a short walk or Uber away are the new shops at City Center, between 9th and 10th Streets, near New York Avenue, NW. Current leases include Hermes, Burberry, Loro Piana, Salvatore Ferragamo, Louis Vuitton, and Morgenthal Frederics. Many are newly opened stores and stack up well to the clientele likely drawn to the new Trump hotel.

Capitol Hill is a big play for the new property. The featured restaurant should set aside several private dining rooms as these are amenities lobbyists and politicians require. A cigar bar could be a popular feature as well. A large, extended bar is a must, with highly experienced bartenders to serve the most discerning politicians, businessmen, and celebrities.

The guest rooms are obligated to be the most modern in sophisticated design with elegant fabrics and furniture including a desk to accommodate several hours of real work along with multiple internet ports and immediate, free wireless. An onsite technician should be available at any hour. A Business Center with the latest equipment to work quickly and efficiently is non-negotiable.

The property should cater to all members of the family including children. While Washington, DC is really a working city, there are venues for kids. Every effort should be made to arrange a room for activities and even an onsite movie theater.

Outlook for the Hotel

Jan A. deRoos, Ph.D., HVS Professor of Hotel Finance and Real Estate at Cornell University explains:

"Washington, DC's luxury hotels are held to a different standard than luxury hotels in most urban cores. Like the entertainment-oriented hotels of Los Angeles, the best hotels in Washington, DC are an important part of the social fabric of the city. Each day, the city's luxury hotels host events of great importance and hotels that take pains to make the physical venue and service standards equal to the event do well; the best of breed understand the importance of their social obligations."

Donald Trump's property occupies a unique location in Washington, DC, a short drive from Capitol Hill and a short walk to all of the museums Washington has to offer. It's worth noting that the museums in Washington are free of charge and open to anyone.

However, the guest profile for this hotel will be someone willing to spend upwards of $400 per night, placing it at the top of the Average Daily Rate (ADR) scale. The high-line hotels mentioned, particularly the Four Seasons and Ritz-Carlton, all run at this price point and maintain robust occupancy rates.

Further, the "group" business custom has returned since the recession and makes up a full 25 percent of the lodging business in the US. Count on major blue-chip associations using this hotel for conferences and meetings despite the lofty pricing. In many cases, the nicer the hotel, the better it reflects on the association. The Trump International Washington, DC will likely be booked by groups years in advance.

One of the leading members of the Saudi Royal Family recently booked the *entire* Four Seasons Hotel in Georgetown for several nights. Was his business primarily in Georgetown? No. The flagship is simply viewed as the finest hotel worldwide by the Saudi's. An entourage of SUV's ferried his Royal Highness to the offices on Capitol Hill to meet lawmakers and to the White House to meet with

President Obama. This is, of course, the guest profile sought by the Trump International Hotel Washington, DC.

Given the aura surrounding Donald Trump and his meteoric rise in the politics, it is likely that this attention will provide plenty of draw on its own, but this will not be part of the operating and marketing strategy.

I imagine a marketing blitz unrivaled by anything seen in Washington, DC or by any other hotel in the city to date. You will see advertisements for the new hotel in every single publication that caters to the wealthy and the major corporate travelers: *Forbes, Fortune, Bloomberg BusinessWeek, Town & Country*, and every single print publication noted for wealthy readership and subscribers such as *The Wall Street Journal* and *The New York Times*.

Add to that a direct, face-to-face sales force that will be quite formidable, professional, polished, and highly experienced. Trump will likely recruit these marketing and sales professionals from other hotels, both around the city and nationally.

Donald Trump himself (if he isn't in the White House) will no doubt be a part of the campaign and include short clips of him touting the hotel, possibly as a lead-in advertisement to news stories or other genre-related in online news and information.

Given the cost of the project, the ADR to be achieved, and the risk associated with a new luxury hotel facing the competitive nature of the hotel market in Washington, DC, this will be a marketing campaign of the first order. When coupled with the fact that the J.W. Marriott, The W Hotel, and The Willard Intercontinental are only a few blocks away, Trump will do everything possible to differentiate his hotel from the others.

While it's easy to say we have the best of everything, the fact remains that the many frequent travelers to the nation's capital who stay in luxury properties tend to become complacent with their choice over the years. Breaking tradition to try something new is sometimes more difficult than it may seem, but Trump will find a way to entice those valued guests.

The international traveler, in particular arriving from the Middle East, the Orient, and others who tend to "overindulge" themselves, will be a high priority for Trump. People like the Saudi Royal who rented the entire Four Seasons Hotel in Georgetown for several days do not look at the room rate. They look at service, food, design, comfort, and security. While they tend to bring their own entourage including security detail, hotel security plays a critical role. Trump is familiar with this type of customer since he is one himself.

Not Just a Developer

Looking across the portfolio of assets that Donald Trump has developed over many years, one word continues to come to mind: Unique.

Whether it is Mar-a-Lago in Palm Beach, the Doral Hotel and Resort (and famous Golf Courses), the storied golf courses in Ireland or finally, the Old Post Office Pavilion conversion in Washington, DC, Donald Trump acquires and develops the dictionary definition of "Trophy Properties."

What exactly is a trophy property? It is a one-of-a-kind, irreplaceable asset, in many cases, known worldwide. Most real estate developers are quite satisfied building properties that make money – period. Donald Trump seeks a profit certainly, and by the success of his projects, he's garnered a very large sum. But it is defined by more than a profit – it's iconic and beyond. When Trump applies his "brand" to an asset, he's applying a layer of operating and marketing expertise that may be the best-known "marque" in the world.

Like it or hate it, you *know* when you've walked into Trump Tower on Fifth Avenue in New York City. Bound by the keynote boutiques of Bergdorf Goodman, Gucci, Tiffany's and Ralph Lauren – and much more – it is not simply an "office building." It is a *monument,* or as close to one as you can get on a busy commercial avenue blending retail, office, and residential uses in one concrete box; a *very well* designed and executed one.

Jan A. deRoos, Ph.D. explains:

"The Trump Organization's commitment to quality, both in the tangible and in the intangibles of service product should serve them well at the "Old Post Office" site. The building provides a backdrop that is second to none; if properly redeveloped, the existing building can be enhanced to serve the needs of guests, dignitaries, social butterflies, those seeking influence and seeking to be influenced. Trump understands the power that a well-designed and appointed space has to serve the mission and influence opinions."

The value of a Trump asset can be assessed using traditional methods. However, those are simply the starting points. Once you recognize that you've just seen a very exceptional property that has no comparison, the basic metrics and calculations serve only as a starting point.

Then you must add in the enormous marketing effort that goes into each and every property in his portfolio. Add in his decades-long experience on *The Apprentice* and his unexpected place in the political spectrum – the Republican nominee for the Presidency of the United States.

If you didn't know who Donald Trump was previously, you certainly know who he is now. Any television, radio station, or internet site will offer up recent appearances, speeches, and massive events promoting his candidacy – *and* his brand.

Make No Mistake

Each time Donald Trump appears on national television, he's promoting vacant office space in his buildings and promoting any unsold condominium units in any of his residential assets; this is a deliberate effort to fill rooms in any of his lodging assets, or encouraging rounds of golf at his elite golf clubs.

But promotion does not equate to valuation and, while Trump has invested millions into the former post office property, the question is whether or not customers pay the price for Trump's premium-branded hotel along Pennsylvania Avenue.

A Look at Valuation

To understand value better, we looked at a number of recent closings on high-end lodging properties in the US. The most notable transaction is the Waldorf Astoria in New York City that sold at a record price of $1.95 billion in 2015. The buyer for the trophy property was Anbang, a Chinese insurance company that owns other high-end properties such as the JW Marriott Essex House near Central Park in Manhattan.

Chinese investors like Anbang have been steady buyers of trophy buildings. According to the *New York Times*, direct investment in the US reached $15.7 billion in 2015. In addition to the Waldorf deal, we looked at other luxury-branded hotels to determine an average price per key of just over $1.5 million.

Trump's DC hotel will have 260 guest rooms, penthouses, and presidential suites. We visited the property and witnessed the transformation of the former postmaster general apartment into a plush presidential suite with the original fireplace and paneling restored. Using the $1.5 million price per key comparable, we have determined that the DC hotel could fetch around $400 million.

Trump has a loan in the amount of $170 million and after subtracting that from the value we arrive at equity of $222 million. If Trump were to score a home run with the DC deal, we could see his worth in the asset exceed $300 million. We consider the debt level moderate, and unless there is another large scale recession, we believe there will be ample revenue to cover the debt service (the loan to value is around 40 percent) and provide Trump with nice dividends along Pennsylvania Avenue.

Similar to Chicago, Las Vegas, and New York, Trump's DC hotel will also serve as an important reminder of the incredible scale of the billionaire's hotel operation. The common ingredients can be summed up in three simple words: luxury, luxury, luxury.

The Trump Factor

TRUMP INTERNATIONAL DC				
Properties	Units	Avg. Key $	$/Sq. Ft.	Totals
Hotel Units	260	$1,508,673	565	$392,254,870
Total				392,254,870
Debt				(170,000,000)
Trump Equity				$222,254,870

CHAPTER 9

MAGNIFICENT MAR-A-LAGO

"Luxury must be comfortable otherwise, it is not luxury."
– Coco Chanel

Mar-a-Lago is Spanish for "Sea to Lake." It's the name of a slim parcel of land in south Florida that is now owned by Donald Trump. The property is strategically clustered across twenty acres that connect the inland waterway known as Lake Worth to the Atlantic Ocean.

Trump has owned the West Palm Beach estate, including the twenty acres of land and existing furniture and fixtures inside, since 1985. He has since added seven other structural amenities along with eight seaside cabanas totaling more than 62,500 square feet.

The estate was purchased in a private sale for an amount that's rumored to be between $10 and $11 million. The actual purchase price for Mar-a-Lago remains somewhat unknown to the public; some sources suggest that Trump paid about $8 million for the real estate, including the contents, and an additional $2 million for a strip of land adjacent to the beach.

Trump didn't just buy a luxurious piece of real estate, he bought a property with a broad reaching historical significance that dates back to 1925, when the original owner and developer, Marjorie Merriweather Post, commenced construction on the spectacular mansion.

Decades before Post invested in Palm Beach, another wealthy investor, Henry Morrison Flagler, began buying up barren real estate in south Florida. He was a high school dropout with incredible business savvy that led him to co-found the Standard Oil Company with John D. Rockefeller in 1870. During a thirty-year period, Flagler invested about $50 million in the railroad, residential homes, and hotel construction, and his innovative successes became the tipping point for entrepreneurial real estate investments in the twentieth century.

During the 1880s, Flagler left New York to forge a second career as *"the father of both Miami and Palm Beach."* He built numerous luxury resorts including the 540-room Ponce de León Hotel, now a part of Flagler College, and the Alcazar hotel, both located in St. Augustine, Florida.

In Palm Beach, Florida, he constructed the 1,100-room Royal Poinciana Hotel on the shores of Lake Worth, adding the Palm Beach Inn on the beach side of the property and eventually renaming it the Breakers Hotel Complex in 1901. In 1897, Flagler opened the Royal Palm Hotel in Miami, Florida.

Flagler passed away in 1913, and about a dozen years later, Marjorie Post traveled by railroad to the highly exclusive town of Palm Beach. Flagler had been the catalyst for the development of the high-end destination that turned into a showcase of wealth.

Post, formerly known as Mrs. E.F. Hutton, was a leading socialite and founder of General Foods, Inc. She was only 27-years-old when her father died and she inherited his fortune including the Post Cereal Company. Post parlayed her $250 million fortune into an empire and invested her wealth in art, jewelry, real estate, and a world-class yacht.

Imagine being 35-years-old and worth millions during the Roaring Twenties. That's when Post decided to build her showcase mansion in West Palm Beach. The U.S. economy was flourishing and anyone with money was living well due to the greatest bull market in American history. The share of wealth controlled by the rich became greater when the Treasury lowered the top marginal income tax rate for the wealthiest Americans from 73 percent to just 25 percent.

In 1927, after spending more than three years planning, designing, and building, Post opened her 118-room princess palace. The Great Depression would hit five years later.

Post must have been very excited to finish building this estate. She used hurricane-resistant concrete and steel to protect the property from natural disasters. The main building was designed by Joseph Urban and Marion Sims Wyeth and provides a variety of architectural elements originating from Italy, Spain, and Portugal. The structure itself was built with Italian stone, about 36,000 fifteenth-century Spanish tiles, and white marble from a Cuban castle.

According to Trump, Post brought in Plus Ultra, or "beyond the ultimate" tiles from Spain, which historians traced back to the 1400s. Trump considered this to be quite the coup.

The grand ballroom is stunning and a winding staircase leads to the second floor where there's a series of coves and hidden bedrooms. The signature element is a 75-foot tower on the main structure. Rumor has it that the cereal heiress would sit on the second-floor balcony and spy on the socialites who visited her estate. She had grandiose taste in the furnishings and accessories that Trump now owns.

Inside the plush mansion are sumptuous carved and gold-plated Italian and French Louis XIV furniture. Trump has also hung a priceless Flemish tapestry that Post cut to fit the wall panels surrounding the enormous living room. A valuable Meissen clock is another showpiece in the room. Post commissioned Florence Ziegfeld's set designer to paint murals along the formal dining room walls that are lit by gorgeous chandeliers. Trump converted the plush library that features a crested fireplace into a cozy bar and sitting area.

During peak season, Post would entertain hundreds of guests at a time, and her staff of 75 would indulge exclusive invitees with perks that included overnight accommodations and transportation by airplane to and from the Mar-a-Lago estate. She would even have her staff wash and repack guests' clothes so that their luggage appeared as if it was just packed.

An Ironic Twist of Ownership

In 1969, the U.S. Department of the Interior designated the estate as a national historic site and the property was entered on the National Register of Historic Places. Post died in 1973, and the property was handed over to the U.S. government for use as a presidential retreat.

In 1983, due to security concerns over the property being surrounded by water and the high cost of maintenance, the government deeded Mar-a-Lago back to the Post Foundation. The pink-and-brown mansion came to be known as a pink elephant and sat empty for years and years, waiting for a buyer.

When the U.S, government owned Mar-a-Lago, only a handful of presidents visited the estate nicknamed the "Southern White House." Richard Nixon toured the property on July 7, 1974, but he wasn't a frequent guest due to him resigning the presidency five months after the Watergate scandal. Jimmy Carter was also rumored to have visited Mar-a-Lago, but the issues of maintenance and possible terrorism risk due to the proximity to Cuba convinced the government to hand the keys back to the Post Estate.

A year later, in 1984, Texan Cerf Stanford Ross made an unsuccessful attempt to nab Mar-a-Lago, but his financing fell apart. Then, in 1985, Donald Trump set his sights on the iconic West Palm trophy. Trump explained:

"On first sight, Mar-a-Lago was like an old beat-up, overgrown Rembrandt waiting to be restored. I came across the wreckage — a fairy-tale castle built by a kindred spirit, the enigmatic and incredibly savvy Marjorie Merriweather Post." Trump went on to say, "Her haunting past echoed through the halls of the palatial estate – in a sense of the theatrical and the invaluable input of Wall Street wizard E.F. Hutton, her husband."

Trump's original visit to Mar-a-Lago wasn't planned. As rumor has it, the billionaire was en route to a dinner party in Palm Beach and asked the chauffeur if there were any good deals in town. According to Trump, the driver said, *"Well, the best thing by far is Mar-a-Lago, but I guess you wouldn't be talking about that."*

Trump skipped the dinner party and drove to the property that was then owned by the Post Estate. He contacted the trustee of the Post Estate and, after a few rounds of negotiations, was able to purchase Mar-a-Lago in December 1985.

There is some mystery regarding Trump's funding of Mar-a-Lago. In Gwenda Blair's book *The Trumps*, she writes:

"The $10 million mortgage contained an unusual proviso by the developer's favorite bank (Chase Bank) that allowed it to go unrecorded." The banker was taking a risk, and the mystery of the mortgage-less deal would later become more obvious ... The developer was able to give the impression that he had forked over the entire purchase price in cash, even though he had paid only $2,811 million out of his pocket."

In 1985, Trump's estimated net worth at the age of 39 was about $600 million, according to *Forbes*. He had been married to his first wife, Ivana Trump, for about eight years and he was looking to extend his foothold in the south. He wanted to provide a lavish playground for his three children, Don Jr., Ivanka, and Eric.

Ivana had already become quite a skilled decorator and she had overseen the renovation of The Plaza Hotel in New York City. Trump and his family enjoyed Mar-a-Lago; the retreat offered a relaxing private getaway for the developer to focus on his tactical wealth building strategies. He wrote his first book, *The Art of the Deal*, at the estate (the book became a *New York Times* bestseller and approximately 3 million copies have been sold to date).

The Plaza Hotel

Trump planned his biggest deal yet by focusing on The Plaza Hotel, while staying at Mar-a-Lago. The southern estate became a powerful tool for Trump to entertain bankers and schmooze them into extending loans that others may have been reluctant to consider. He was able to lure the bankers into a captive compound to negotiate bigger deals.

Trump bought The Plaza in 1988 at the peak of the market when he convinced bankers, led by Citibank, to loan him $425 million. While Mar-a-Lago was a fraction of the excessive price paid to buy The Plaza, Trump's estimated $10 million investment in Palm Beach served as an incredible negotiating tool with which he could convince bankers that he was the next big developer in south Florida.

According to Trump, when his first offer of $28 million was turned down, he decided to play hardball. He insinuated he had bought the beachfront property directly in front of it through a third party and he planned to put up a hideous home to block its ocean view.

"That was my first wall," he said. "That drove everybody nuts. They couldn't sell the big house because I owned the beach, so the price kept going down and down."

In the end, Trump bought the landmark in 1985 for a bargain, paying an estimated $5 million for the house and $3 million for Post's antiques and lavish furnishings.

By 1988, Trump began to feel the power of success, and although the $10 million signature loan he signed in 1985 to purchase Mar-a-Lago was pocket change in comparison to other purchases, the $125 million personal guarantee to buy The Plaza was a sign that Trump was taking elevated risks. (It appears that Trump actually pocketed $2 million on the purchase).

Bankers Kept Lending, Trump Kept Building

By 1990 though, (as discussed in chapter 1), Trump became overleveraged, and because he had personally guaranteed loans with Citibank, many of his trophies were underwater.

As Mark Singer in *The New Yorker* wrote:

"Excessively friendly bankers infected with the promiscuous optimism that made the eighties so memorable and so forgettable had financed Trump's acquisitive impulses to the tune of three billion, seven hundred and fifty million dollars."

Trump had personally guaranteed almost $1 billion and many of his properties were not cash flowing. In addition to risks associated with The Plaza Hotel, Trump had also been subjected to high-stakes gambling in the form of three casinos in Atlantic City.

The oasis, once a family retreat in south Florida, became the war room for Trump to negotiate and strategize about his next steps. Trump wrote in his book *Never Give Up*, *"Mar-a-Lago felt like a minor weight to me."* What had once been the entertainment mecca was now a domicile for Trump to escape from the New York City madness.

In 1989, *Forbes* ranked Trump's wealth at $1.7 billion, making him one of America's 20 richest people. In 1990, however, *Forbes* ran a cover story estimating Trump's wealth to be only about $500 million.

As the chips started to fall, Trump explained in the book, *Trump Never Give Up: How I Turned My Biggest Challenges in Success:*

"I remember being in a room full of bankers, trying to work out a very complex situation, and they were friends who were truly trying to be helpful."

Trump, having grown so accustomed to frequent flyovers, recounted commenting during the meeting:

"Since it's Friday, I think I'll go down to Mar-a-Lago for the weekend on my 727."

According to Trump, the bankers didn't see any humor in the hype, especially since he was on the hook for millions and they expected him to make good on his personal guarantees.

He began thinking about how he could monetize the private mansion without losing control of it. He had already lost substantial wealth because of high leverage, and by converting Mar-a-Lago to an income-producing asset, he would be able to appease the bankers by creating a unique cash flow vehicle.

In the course of Trump's negotiations with bankers, he was able to extinguish a large portion of his personal debts and save Mar-a-Lago. He initially planned to monetize the club by subdividing the land into 14 lots while preserving the primary house with the intention of selling the lots. The City of Palm Beach suggested an alternate plan to the developer to subdivide the property into eight lots instead.

Trump felt like he was being "bamboozled" by the city and that he was entitled by law to 14 subdivision lots. He said, *"It was totally unfair."* He filed a $100 million lawsuit against the city, and during the litigation, the town offered to allow Trump to divide the estate into 14 lots. He rebuffed and said, *"I told them I wasn't interested anymore."* Trump decided that he now wanted to monetize the deal with a private club structure.

Former Palm Beach attorney Paul Rampell said about the case:

"The expense of Mar-A-Lago has got to shift from one person to a group of people. At this time, more support has been expressed for the idea of a private club than for a museum or for subdividing. It's a community issue. It isn't just the perceived problem of Donald Trump."

In April of 1995, Mar-a-Lago became The Mar-a-Lago Club. As of 2016, the property is the last remaining Palm Beach estate with buildings and land maintained in almost their original conception. Ever since Trump's thorough restoration began in 1985, the Mar-a-Lago project has been a work in progress.

The winter of 1995 was Mar-a-Lago's first full season as a commercial enterprise. The initiation fee for the private club was $25,000. The fee later rose to $50,000, then $100,000, and is now quoted at $200,000.

Over the last two decades, Trump has invested millions into Mar-a-Lago, more recently a 20,000 square foot Louis XIV ballroom that opened in 2005, where Trump married his third wife, Melania. The Versailles-like ballroom, named the Donald J. Trump Grand Ballroom, has a lavish exhibition of mirrors, marble, gold, and seventeen Austrian crystal chandeliers. It's the largest ballroom on the island.

Post's original ballroom was not big or grand enough for Trump and, while the cereal baroness enjoyed square dancing in close quarters (popular in the roaring twenties), Trump opted for a much larger facility to be used by a long list of celebrities viewed on *Life Styles of the Rich and Famous.*

He has invited many high-profile guests such as Michael Jackson to stay overnight. It was once rumored that Princess Diana and Madonna were members but that could not be verified and was likely a promotional tactic to build buzz. When I visited the club in November 2014, I met Regis Philbin at Mar-a-Lago.

Rumor has it that Trump spent $100,000 on four gold-plated bathroom sinks near the ballroom. The grounds on Mar-a-Lago are immaculate and Trump had the hedge on South Ocean Drive chopped down to ensure passersby could see his castle.

"It's become part of the fabric of the social life of Palm Beach," said Jane Day who, as the town's historic preservation consultant, at times clashed with Trump. But like many, she credited Trump with saving the historic home and managing it in a way that has allowed many people to enjoy it.

The property employs a staff of waiters, landscapers, cooks and others, including foreign workers brought in using special visas. Trump's reliance on immigrant labor has received attention in recent months as he has made illegal immigration a signature issue on the campaign trail.

Trump's most valuable employee at Mar-a-Lago is Bernd Lembcke who serves as the Managing Director & Executive Vice President at Mar-a-Lago. He has been with Mr. Trump for over a decade.

Trump said in his book, *Think Like a Billionaire,* that Melanie loves Mar-a-Lago more than any other place, including the South of France, Portofino, Lake Como, and other beautiful places in Europe.

The long list of members and guests who have stayed at Mar-a-Lago include Henry Kissinger, Elizabeth Taylor, Oprah, and Celine Dion. Trump's son, Eric, was married to Lara Yunaska at Mar-a-Lago in 2014. One former member and well-known real estate icon, Alfred Taubman, passed away in 2015, and his son, Bobby Taubman (now CEO of Taubman Centers) explains the club's lure:

"Like many of Donald's assets, Mar-a-Lago is completely unique, that he combines with his sense of service and professionalism, which together are implicitly the (globally renowned) Trump brand."

What's It All Worth

I have visited Mar-a-Lago on multiple occasions, and I consider the 88-year-old property to be one of the finest gems in the Trump real estate portfolio. The 18-acre parcel of land is irreplaceable, and while Trump could have converted the land to a subdivision, I believe the highest and best use is precisely what Trump had in mind.

By selling club memberships, Trump generates sustainable cash flow that produces very predictable profits. I suspect that Trump's private estate has more than 200 exclusive members to date and according to Trump's Federal Election Commission (FEC) filings, generates over $15 million annually.

In terms of overall quality, Mar-a-Lago offers the very best amenities and customer service imaginable. Just as Marjorie Merriweather Post intended, Mar-a-Lago is a playground for the rich and famous and the club is uniquely positioned to provide a certain level of influence and prestige. On one of my visits, there were a dozen luxury brand cars parked in the driveway such as a new Rolls-Royce Phantom retailing around $400,000. In other words, the fees for being a member of Mar-a-Lago are pocket change.

The Mar-a-Lago halls exhibit Trump's deep-rooted appreciation for fine architecture, quality craftsmanship, art, and antiques. Like most of his properties, he has decorated the home with crystal, marble, and gold, which are ostensibly his favorite investment class outside of the actual real estate that he owns.

There are least eight different types of marble within the property and his demand for perfectionism does not go unnoticed in the elaborate decorations in the ballroom. To the average person, the 24-karat gold leaf ceilings would be mistaken for faux gold leaf, but Trump held nothing back when putting his "Post-like" stamp on perfection above the walls at a cost of at least $7 million.

From the opulent mahogany paneling in the spa to the superb Italian marble and the sparkling Austrian crystal chandeliers, Trump simply does not cut corners. His top lieutenant at Mar-a-Lago, Bernd Lembcke said:

"Mr. Trump didn't want to change the main house as it is such a historic architectural treasure and after the house was vacant for eight years, he was determined to bring it back to life and maintain its integrity in the process."

Approaching a Mar-a-Largo Valuation

Trump paid around $10 million for Mar-a-Lago 20 years ago and the billionaire has invested several million dollars since then. Given his global brand reach, we suspect that the membership requests at Mar-a-Lago have increased quite a bit; however, we consider the cost approach to valuation more meaningful. In other words, we believe that a very wealthy investor would be willing to pay a large sum if Trump ever decided to monetize the trophy asset.

The site on which Mar-a-Lago sits is considered the most valuable parcel of land in south Florida and the land value itself is likely worth about $50 million. The multiple structures and world-class amenities include European indoor and terrace dining, oceanfront swimming pool and Beach Club, Trump Spa and Salon, six championship tennis courts, and a full-size croquet court. A chip and putt golf course, a state of the art fitness center, and the coveted Donald J. Trump ballroom could easily fetch at least $225 million.

The post-depression furniture, art, and accessories are matchless, but for the sake of valuation, I would put at least $25 million on the antique collection. Therefore, our combined value of Mar-a-Lago is $300 million with no property-level debt recorded.

Arguably, few U.S. investors could afford to own such a unique property; however, I suspect there are plenty of international investors who could easily purchase this southern piece of paradise. The most well-heeled investors can enjoy the facilities to entertain guests or relax by the oceanside pool by joining the ultra-exclusive club.

One of my most cherished experiences at Mar-a-Lago was when I introduced my family to Mr. Trump. It was Thanksgiving Day in November 2014 and we were all sitting outside for lunch. My youngest daughter, A.J., yelled out *"That's Donald Trump!"* Of course, everyone heard her scream his name, including Trump. He walked over to the table and I introduced my entire family. Since then, I have been around Trump at least a dozen times and he *always* asks me how my family is doing.

There is no other way to describe Mar-a-Lago or Donald Trump than to use the words, "blue chip." As I said, I will never forget the encounter at Mar-a-Lago and the attention to detail, both in terms of the property characteristics as well as Donald Trump's attention to people.

Donald Trump has set the bar very high and Mar-a-Lago is perhaps one of the finest examples of Trump's brand equity, which is the intersection of his vast real estate reach and his luxury branding message. Much like Marjorie Post, Trump uses this iconic asset to wine and dine the most elite guests, and in turn, the luxurious Mar-a-Lago mansion affirms to the world that Trump's biggest competitive advantage is wealth creation.

Mar-a-Lago is a symbol of Trump's prosperity and resilience; by hanging onto it through the toughest of times it has become a physical representation of his mental blueprint to success.

The Mar-a-Lago fortress has stood through multiple economic cycles, and the "sea to lake" moat promises enduring brand strength.

By combining Trump's superior real estate acumen and his Post-like social skills, the magnificence of Palm Beach commands premium pricing for what is truly a uniquely exceptional asset. Bernd Lembcke adds:

"Mr. Trump left his footprint, and it is quite obvious that he brought Mar-a-Lago back to life."

The Trump Factor

MAR-A-LAGO			
Properties	.	.	Totals
Land Value			$50,000,000
Building Improvements			225,000,000
Accessories, Art			25,000,000
Total			300,000,000
Debt			$0
Trump Equity			$300,000,000

CHAPTER 10

TRUMP IS THE "FOUR SEASONS HOTEL CHAIN" OF GOLF

It is extremely difficult to value many of Trump's golf clubs because the company is private and does not disclose details normally obtained with publicly-traded golf club owners like Club Corporation (NYSE: MYCC).

There is no substantial or standardized industry data on golf course valuation; however, we contacted a leading industry expert to assist us with this ever-increasing sector of Trump's global real estate empire. Steven M. Ekovich is the National Managing Director and First Vice President of the Leisure Investment Properties Group for Marcus and Millichap. He has been involved in over $3.5 billion in commercial real estate transactions over the last 25 years.

The Leisure Properties Group, which advises on private and public golf courses, golf resorts, golf master planned communities (golf courses with additional lots and land to sell in addition to the golf asset), and marinas, has sold 85 golf assets in the last few years in addition to underwriting approximately $2 billion in golf assets.

They have sold to, and sold for, every major golf lender who traded assets through the recession including most of the major golf owners in the US and around the world like Trump, Club Corporation, and ClubLink, as well as international buyers from Canada, Asia, and Europe.

In addition to being quoted in *Golf Inc.*, *The New York Times*, *Bloomberg*, and numerous other publications as experts on golf valuation and sales, Mr. Ekovich was also a part of Bryant Gumbel's *Real Sports* exposé on golf, which aired in 2014. He was instrumental in closing two recent golf portfolios and his expertise and reputation in the golf course business is stellar.

Complexity of Golf Course Valuations

When valuing golf courses, Ekovich insists that many inexperienced analysts, appraisers, and investors compare golf courses with other core asset classes like shopping centers and office buildings. An apartment building, office, retail center, or industrial building in a town or city can be valued by price per unit or price per square foot because the assets are interchangeable.

The general footprint for similar product types is the same. For example, a big box space is the same in retail, a 1500 square foot apartment is the same no matter the builder; a high cube bulk warehouse of 200,000 square feet completed to a vanilla shell is essentially the same except for some differences in build-out.

Tell me the product type, the city, and the size, and any appraiser can give you the price per square foot or per unit. However, our golf analyst explains that there are no two clubs that are identical and, therefore, it's foolish to use a price per acre or price per hole like one would do in a commercial real estate valuation as a data set to compare one golf course against another.

Ekovich says it is not possible to compare two golf courses within a mile of each other if both, for example, are private, but one has a 30,000 square foot clubhouse and the other a 15,000 square foot clubhouse, one is on 300 acres and the other is on 150 acres, one has rolling terrain (which is more expensive to maintain than a flat course), one has initiation fees of $100k and the other has none, and one has a pool while the other doesn't; the list goes on and on.

Ekovich argues that the best way to measure a golf club's value is based on operating metrics. While many appraisers use a discounted cash flow based on a five or seven-year pro forma, they make up numbers the course may achieve like, "*The course which now has 150 members will have 250 in five years,"* and these members are going to descend from where – *heaven?*

Then they discount those values to arrive at a precedent value and say, *"If the club hit our pro forma, it would be worth this value."* (However, the club doesn't have 250 members; it has 150 members, so the value is a made-up number with no basis in today's reality.)

Another method they use is the price per acre and price per hole all of which are about as useful to a buyer of golf assets as the price per nematode. (Every golf owner hates parasitic worms.)

Ekovich is quick to point out that while 80 percent of the time their group has to explain to owners, banks, and buyers why the appraisal is wholly inaccurate, there is a small cadre of great golf appraisers, some with the Society of Golf Appraisers (SGA) designation and some without, both who consult with his group and other golf advisors regularly, who can accurately value golf assets.

He says buyers use valuation metrics like the gross revenue multiplier, EBITDA multiple (Earnings Before Interest, Taxes, Depreciation, and Amortization). EBITDA is a multiple of cash flow without debt service or tax deductions (similar to capitalization rates) but is the inverse of cap rates.

For example: a 9x EBITDA Multiplier (EBITDA of $500,000) provides a price of $4,500,000. The cap rate is the inverse so divide 9 into 100 and your cap rate is 11.11. To calculate the price using the cap rate, take the $500,000 in EBITDA and divide by 11.11 percent and you get $4,500,000.

The reason for this discussion of cap rates and EBITDA multiples is to show valuing a golf asset is not purely a real estate valuation which generally uses price per foot and cap rates, it is also a business sale with enterprise value.

One buyer will talk about EBITDA multiples and the other buyer will discuss cap rates depending on whether the person is more real estate oriented or golf business oriented. Very sophisticated buyers also use Internal Rate of Return (IRR), but that is beyond the scope of this book.

Valuation of Trump's Portfolio

In valuing Trump's golf portfolio, we have opted to utilize the gross revenue multiplier since we have a baseline of data that was provided within Donald Trump's Federal Election Filings (FEC). Since businesses are competitive and the businesses Trump owns are private, we don't know the EBITDA multiples for those assets, which in most cases would provide the most accurate valuation method.

Ekovich explained that gross revenue multiples, (GRMs) range from .65x (a poor property) with a negative EBITDA to 2.0x (a good private course well located in a major metro area) and stated that the outliers – the "super special" courses, signature designers, high revenue, irreplaceable real estate in major metros could be closer to 3.0x or even higher.

One note to the valuation of Trump's portfolio on the golf metrics side: a number of his clubs, like Doral (Chapter 12), have large hospitality components thrown into the gross income number that was reported in the filing. For those cases, an investor or appraiser would not use the same valuation metrics as are used for the courses, making the commingled incomes using a GRM multiplier even more inaccurate.

What Ekovich meant is that there are special golf assets that are irreplaceable with exceptional demographics and a regional, local, or international brand. When asking the golf expert whether or not Trump's clubs commanded the special premium he said:

"He (Trump) buys irreplaceable land, with incredible views, in major metros, adds value through his reinvention capital and the Trump brand. No one buys real estate that doesn't think about the highest and best uses. He (Trump) is no fool."

What he says is quite simple: golf devalues real estate versus alternative uses when the asset is located in infill locations. Think about it. Does growing grass in a crowded major metro location add more value to the community than building houses, hotels, or shopping centers?

Ekovich noted that many golf courses are zoned agricultural or deed restricted and can't be developed unless the future land plan can be changed. This means the municipality would have to agree it is in the best interests of the community.

You only have to look around the country to see golf assets being sold to developers for two to six times what they are worth as golf courses. As an example, Ekovich notes he has a golf course in upstate New York under contract for four times what the course is worth as an operating golf course.

This doesn't mean Trump has plans today or ever to convert the courses to housing or other uses as some may be zoning or deed restricted and would need the town governing bodies to agree to allow another use. Whether you are Sam Zell, Carl Icahn or Donald Trump, you still have to look at all your options when you buy real estate especially if a particular use may fail in that location. Every astute real estate investor uses this thought process.

The Three-Legged Stool

When we look at the Trump golf portfolio, Ekovich posits the valuation is like a three-legged stool. The first leg is for the metrics, in this case the GRM, the second leg is for "highest and best use" land value, and the third is for the brand. Certainly, Ekovich maintains that you could use a crude rule of thumb of 3x gross revenues but that could be way off for the reasons cited above; golf assets aren't interchangeable.

Next, how can one account for irreplaceable land value? There is value over and above the value of the operating golf asset that can be attributed to the land. If for example, there is excess land to build on, if you can take 9 holes or 18 holes out of play, or you close the whole course because of favorable zoning, there is tremendous value there. You can't diminish the impact of the land value over and above the golf value on some of Trump's assets.

Finally, Ekovich notes, the third leg of the Trump stool of valuation is the Trump brand.

In golf today, how many ownership brands can you name? There are both large golf owners and golf management companies that do a phenomenal job, but how many times do people use the name of the management company or owner when they talk about playing the course? Robert Dedman, founder of ClubCorp, wanted to keep the course's name prominent and his company in the background for a number of sound business reasons. That is also the case with Kemper and Troon.

However, there are exceptions like Troon's course called Troon North and Kemper has the Kemper Open. Even though these large owners and management companies put out great product, in general, the brand strength is not like Trump's.

On the other hand, Trump took his hotel brand, casino brand, and real estate brand and boldly stepped where others have not, using his name on the marquee of every course. The normal discourse we hear from people playing a course is, "*I am playing at Three Rivers Country Club today*", not "*at XYZ Management Company's course.*"

Golfers will play a Trump course and tell their friends, "*I am going to play Trump National NJ, FL*", etc., and pay more for the expected five-star treatment they receive at a Trump course. *Trump is the Four Seasons Hotel Chain of golf.* You always know you will receive the highest standard of club experience, from the course and clubhouse design to the hospitality component.

What is Trump's brand worth? Apple and Starbucks have a brand, and in their financial statements, there is undoubtedly an entry for goodwill. One might say if Trump sold his course, the brand would go away. That is true but then Trump could license his name as he has done before.

So there you have it. If we can take the 3x multiple as a crude measure of value, we may be close to value with a number of the courses, but as a portfolio, we may be way off base because of the other two valuation legs to the stool, "highest and best use" for the land part of the valuation and the brand value contribution to worth.

Some would argue the brand is baked into the income if you use the income method and that would be true, but it explains why the multiples would need to be higher on Trump's courses and choosing the correct multiple is where the art form comes into the valuation process to get it right.

The question people should be asking, according to Ekovich is, whether the values in Trump's portfolio or any golf portfolio are sustainable. We have heard golf is a dying sport and the press has been eager to report golf foreclosures and residents hysterical about losing their course when the owner shuts it down. So Mr. Ekovich, is the sky falling on golf? In particular, is the sky falling on Trump's portfolio?

Ekovich says his research department, headed by Raymond Demby, puts out a publication entitled, *The Semi-Annual Golf & Resort Investment Report*. In 2012, the Report forecasted a change in direction from six years of golf fundamentals decline in rounds, revenue, EBITDA and property values.

The media and golf pundits alike were decreeing golf's demise in 2012; however, the LIPG's research and internal metrics led them to state in their 2012 issue that the golf market is turning around. As they forecasted in 2013, golf financial fundaments started to show visible signs not only of stopping the incessant decline in fundaments, but actually showed signs of the impending turnaround. (The historical reports from the LIPG are on its website www. leisurepropertiesgroup.com)

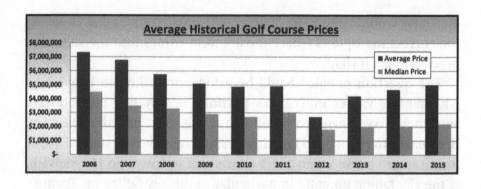

As you can see from the chart above, his group forecasted correctly. After six years of declines in value, both golf's average price and median price rebounded and has done so for three consecutive years. The following quote was pulled from the *2015 Year in Review*:

> *"With rounds and revenue both up for the third year in a row, (aided by a few more golfing days, better expense management, course closings, and consumer's growing pocketbooks), it is time to officially declare "we are in a changed golf market."*

For the third straight year, both the average and median golf course values are up. *What is causing these trends?* Job growth, tighter labor market conditions, expanding payrolls, and a volatile stock market are all factors which are major contributors to elevating both golf's operational performance and property values. These positive factors affect not only golf, but the entire US real estate market and led to the first increase in interest rates in nine years. That small interest rate increase is not expected to hurt golf values.

Golf Trends Returning to "Normal"

It's becoming clearer that the golf market is stabilizing and a healthier US economy continues to affect golf in positive ways. Increased employment and earnings have caused an increase in consumer spending; some of that is bound to go towards golf. Improved operating fundamentals, increased demand from a growing economy, and reduced competition due to course closures all lead to expanding revenue and EBITDA for golf course owners over time.

This improved performance has meant fewer distressed properties in the market and more buyers from outside of the industry driving property values higher. Trump bought a significant portion of his portfolio during the recession and now he is riding the wave of increasing golf values. He was prescient in buying at the bottom of the market, structuring great deals, and improving the assets going into the rise in golf's values.

Ekovich says Trump buys smart; he buys deals and does not tend to get emotional over a deal and overpay. Ekovich sold Trump the Ritz Carlton, now known as Trump National Jupiter.

Mr. Trump told Ekovich: *"You know I bought Doral."*
Ekovich replied: *"Yes, but I don't know if you got a deal or not."*
Trump said: *"I paid $150M and the previous owner paid $500M."*
Ekovich agreed: *"It sounds like you not only got a good deal but a good steal."*

Ekovich said the Ritz Carlton Golf club was a very complex transaction because the Ritz Club and single family homes were being split from the golf asset and all services were shared. Eric Trump did 80 percent of the negotiating and was incredible to deal with; he had a quick mind, a deal-maker mentality, was gracious and very creative.

With core commercial real estate cap rate compression, buyers are now chasing yield in non-core assets and golf is one of those assets. As this happens, traditional buyers will need to adjust if they want to acquire more golf assets and compete with the new wave of investors.

What Ekovich is saying is the distress is gone in the market, golf is more normalized, and with more buyers vying for golf assets, values will continue to increase, which of course help's Trump's portfolio.

There is also the matter of golf industry participation. Everyone knows golf's participation is down. But why and, as some have questioned, will it get worse?

The National Golf Foundation's (NGF) data shows that, in the last two years, golf participation is leveling out in the 24.5 to 25 million range. Ekovich says he attended the NGF summit in San Diego. After a copious amount of research was presented, the NGF came up with a very interesting theory.

Some golf pundits think golf participation is in a slow spiral down, but the NGF has a plausible theory about why it won't continue. The NGF believes that at the height of golf's participation in 2005, we had three to four stimulants affecting golf causing a temporary "Bubble Effect":

Golf Participation in the U.S.
(Number of U.S. Golfers in Millions)

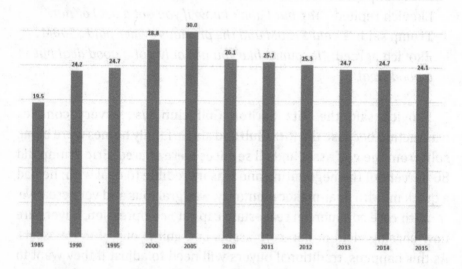

With the crash of Tiger Woods, the stock market, and housing values, the extra five million golfers we had at the height of the market (30 million), were not really committed golfers, but instead, casual golfers spurred to take up golf or try it as a result of the three aforementioned effects. The NGF believes participation will not fall much below where we are today because this is the real normal level of where golf participation was 20 years ago (and where it would have remained, if not for the "bubble" factors).

If this is true, we will continue to shed more functionally obsolete golf courses (those poorly located and/or poorly run), and we will move back into an equilibrium with the nearly 25 million golfers we have now.

When supply and demand are more or less back in balance, as the population grows, rounds will eventually begin to climb again with revenue and golf values to ride the wave. Now we have established that golf values are going up, operational fundamentals are getting a little better, and the stabilization of golf participants looks like it is going to be around 25 million golfers.

Who else believes the golf market is going to be better? Golf's landscape has been forever changed by six mega deals that transacted in 2014. According to Ekovich, when nearly a *billion* trades hands in the golf market, affecting almost 10 percent of the stock, that capital brings with it two side benefits: the ability to infuse more funds into capital projects for courses in need and a significantly reduced capital-to-debt basis for investors.

If you look at the golf industry as a patient who has had the six-year flu, this billion-dollar infusion is like receiving the most powerful penicillin known to mankind. What does this mean going forward? To answer that question, look at the major golf course transaction data from 2014 below.

| ClubCorp went Public: Raised $168.8m | ClubCorp Acquired Sequoia: $265m for 30 Courses, 17 Management Contracts and 3 Leases | Kohlberg and Co Acquired Majority Interest in Troon | Arcis Equity Acquired CNL Portfolio: $306.5m for 46 Golf Courses | New Castle Investments Acquired American Golf for $219m | C-Bons Acquired Walton Street Portfolio (Price is Confidential): 26 Golf Courses |

A lot of educated people who are stakeholders in the industry are putting their money where their mouths are now. According to Ekovich, what he has seen in the last 25 years is that all of the financial and market factors can't always be accounted for in the *"math models when forecasting where the market is going."*

Sometimes you have to add into the equation other influences like what you can learn from historical events in other industries or major events that affect the subject industry which are not already known. These include future demographic shifts and industry innovations.

For example, a new golf phenomenon like Jordan Spieth or Jason Day could emerge to create increased golf interest in younger players and new inventions such as four-wheeled scooters that look like skateboards and carry your clubs as you surf around the course now available at many clubs or even hovercrafts can make playing golf more fun. In addition, millennials' careers are becoming more stable at the same time we have 70 million baby-boomers retiring.

There has been almost a billion dollars in 2014 in portfolio sales or private (PE) infusions which are betting on the golf industry. Ekovich said he is not being blind with denial and saying golf doesn't have its share of issues, because they are well documented.

However, with all the things we discussed (closing/repurposing of 150 courses per year, improved operating fundamentals and economies of scale, market consolidation, lower debt/capital basis, stabilizing course utilization, etc.), it looks and feels like the industry is healthier and should continue to become even more healthy in the future.

Trump's golf portfolio was bought at the right time, he cut great deals, he puts millions back into reinvention capital and hires the best of the industry's professionals to create his signature real estate assets. He runs to the highest standard in the industry and the emerging golf market will continue to help the value of his assets. Now let's examine them in more detail.

CHAPTER 11

TRUMP GOLF

"Greatness is talent applied consistently."
– Gary Player

As any golfer will tell you, the sport is about consistency. The way to become consistent is through the commitment to goals and the discipline to attain them. Discipline is part of Trump's blueprint. If you have the desire to accomplish something, discipline comes easily.

Donald Trump loves golf and his passion for the game is rooted in mental and physical abilities learned early in life. As a young boy, he loved sports. While attending high school at New York Military Academy, he was a member of the varsity soccer, baseball, and football teams. He won numerous awards including one for athletic performance in 1960.

Trump excelled in baseball, a game requiring rigorous mental and physical practice. Being good at baseball and golf involves skills based on routine consistency. While attending high school at NYMA, Trump became the captain of the baseball team and, in 1964, as a senior, was scouted professionally by the Boston Red Sox. Trump knew he wanted to be a successful investor, not a professional athlete, and enrolled in the Bronx's Fordham University before transferring to the Wharton School at the University of Pennsylvania.

While at Wharton, Trump shifted from baseball to golf. In an interview with *Golf Digest* in 2013 he said:

"I was going to the Wharton School of finance, at the University of Pennsylvania, and I had friends that were golfers. I'd never played golf – I always played baseball and football and stuff."

Trump was a self-taught golfer. He had played a few rounds with his dad growing up (Chapter 12, Doral), but his passion for winning was the biggest motivator for learning the sport. He explained:

"I'd go out to Cobbs Creak, in Philadelphia, yeah, a public course, a rough course, no grass on the tees, no nothing, but it was good, and great people. All hustlers out there. I mean, more hustlers than any place I've seen to this day. I played golf with my friends, and then I started to play with the hustlers. And I learned a lot. I learned about golf, I learned about gambling. I learned about everything."

Trump's very first round was in Newport, Rhode Island and he explained his lesson in golf etiquette:

"I'll never forget it – I was playing right behind the Auchincloss family New York philanthropists who owned one of Newport's famous mansions, (the Hammersmith Farm), and I knew nothing about golf, so I kept hitting balls into them. Which did not play well in Newport. They kept looking around: 'Who in the hell is hitting balls into us?'"

Trump's passion for golf and his background in real estate finance became complimentary attributes. He explained:

"I sorta got into the business by accident. I started off in Palm Beach. It's complicated, but essentially I won that land in a lawsuit, 600 acres, and I said, 'What am I gonna do now'? And I said, 'I'm gonna build a great golf course'. And that's what I did."

Trump International West Palm Beach

In 1996, Palm Beach County agreed to lease Trump roughly 215 acres near the corner of Summit and Congress Avenue in suburban West Palm Beach after agreeing to drop a $75 million lawsuit over airplane noise at his Mar-a-Lago club located there (Chapter 9). According to sources, Trump pays the county $527,000 a year to lease the land and the money is used to operate that same airport.

In 2002, the county agreed to lease Trump an adjacent 62-acre site for around $293,000 plus 10 percent non-compounding interest annually. The market value of both sites is $13.6 million according to the Palm Beach County Property Appraiser's Office.

The two ground leases don't expire until 2074 and restrict the use of the land to a golf facility. In an interview, Trump recalls:

"So I sued the county. They wound up settling, and I got 350 incredible acres - the land that's now Trump International Golf Club (An attorney for Palm Beach County says the settlement was unrelated to the land). Which has a quite expensive exit from the highway, by the way. The state's spending $400 million on a highway (widening and improving interstate 95), but didn't build me an exit, and I put up quite a fuss about that. They ended up building a $30 million exit (Florida Department of Transportation says the exit cost $40 million) that goes to my $45 million course."

Trump opened the 18-hole course in the fall of 1999. Excluding the leased land, Trump invested over $40 million in designing and constructing the course and luxury amenities. The prestigious West Palm Club is just minutes away from Mar-a-Lago and listed by *Golf Digest* as one of the 50 Best New Golf Clubs built in the United States. It is also rated as the #1 course in the state of Florida and ranked sixth nationally by *Golf Magazine*.

The Championship course has hosted nine LPGA tour Championships with winners such as Annika Sorenstam, Karri Webb and Lorena Ochoa and two ADT Skills Challenges won by Nick Faldo and Peter Jacobson. The practice facility is so highly regarded that many professionals from the PGA, LPGA, and Champions tours regularly visit to practice during the off-season. According to designer Jim Fazio, this project is *"an architect's dream come true."*

When first visiting the course, we were startled by the extravagant landscaping capturing a near theme park ambiance. The perimeter of the course, ringed with over 700 mature Royal Palms, defines the boundaries and makes the club setting feel like a private estate. Meticulously maintained tropical plants and palms were breathtaking as waterfall and topographical features completed a sense of paradise.

Over three million cubic yards of earth were moved over nine months, some being used to create the highest golf elevation in the state of Florida at 58 feet above sea level. The result is a landscape unique to the South including a live oak forest highlighted with tropical plants and palms characteristic of the region.

When Donald Trump envisioned his first golf investment, he dreamed of one that would complement the luxurious standards of his nearby residence. Trump International West Palm Beach is a world-class course comprised of elements unlike any other.

It was Trump's desire to create the best golf course that could be built and his mental blueprint became reality. At the end of the book, I will rate the courses and all of Trump's properties and I can assure you that this golf club is something uniquely special!

Trump National Westchester

When Donald Trump purchased the 147-acre property in Westchester New York, formerly known as Briar Hall Country Club, his goal was to create a mirror-image of the course in West Palm Beach, both irreplaceable and valued at a premium.

Recognizing a good deal under foreclosure, Trump purchased the golf course for $8 million in 1997 and bulldozed it in 1999. After years of delays due to zoning and permitting, he renamed his second club, Trump National Westchester, and opened on April 15, 2002.

At the time, Trump said he spent $40 million to build the course designed by architect Jim Fazio. Later sources indicate that Trump spent almost $60 million and about $7 million of it went into one of the shortest golf holes with a waterfall backdrop.

The par-72 course plays extremely long, a distance of 7,244 yards from the back tees flowing naturally over the contours of the hilly terrain. Fairways and greens are nestled around ridges and swales, fitting naturally into the land. Large, scalloped bunkers of fine, white sand are meticulously manicured, seemingly artificial as I toured the grounds.

The amenities of "Trump-turesque" include the 42,000 square foot clubhouse with a pro shop, card rooms, and a fitness center with full-service locker rooms including massage rooms and exercise equipment. There is also an outdoor swimming pool with heated whirlpool spa and four tennis courts.

Trump National Golf Club Bedminster

After creating his first two golf courses, Trump decided to acquire another location which became known as Trump National Golf Club Bedminster in New Jersey.

Records show that Trump bought the Briarcliff Manor site and Briar Hall Golf and Country Club in 2002 for around $35 million. It was a down market and Trump purchased the distressed asset at a deep discount from National Fairways, a Connecticut-based golf course developer that had acquired it from automaker DeLorean at a bankruptcy auction in early 2000.

National Fairways had proposed to convert the estate into an exclusive country club featuring an 18-hole golf course, swimming pool, equestrian facilities, tennis and paddle courts. The Georgian-style red brick manor house was the intended clubhouse surrounded by 14 single-family building lots. Trump said at the time:

"Those people had a great vision but didn't quite have the funding."

Although Trump was not established yet as a multi-club golf owner, he stated:

"I have no problem getting members. They know what kind of work I do. What's been proven in Florida and Westchester County is if you build a great course, the people will come."

Located on about 520 acres, the first nine holes opened on April 15, 2004, and Trump recalls spending over $40 million to complete the Trump National as designed by golf course architect, Jim Fazio, creator of Trump International in West Palm Beach.

All of the Trump golf courses incorporate trademark elements and Bedminster's is the 13th hole waterfall, a 101-foot high cliff of black granite with overflowing water at the rear of the green. Trump purposely designed the breathtaking water feature to amaze members and guests and it worked.

I was astonished to see huge greens patterned similar to the Augusta National Golf Club. There are also enormous Trump-made lakes and creeks flowing throughout the course. It's hard to imagine you are just an hour from New York City as you witness the spectacular views of northern Westchester.

Similarly, I was stunned to see the fleet of luxury cars parked in the driveway, evidence of very affluent members with annual fees of $300,000. Previous and current members include Bill Clinton, Rudy Giuliani, and Joe Torre. In 2005, *Golf Magazine* ranked the course #73 in the US and #84 by *Golf Digest* for 2005 and 2006. Also, the club hosted Ivanka Trump and Jared Kushner's wedding in October 2009.

With a golf club portfolio anchored by three exceptional golf clubs, Trump was ready to begin scaling his golf operations by capitalizing on his experience and investing in troubled country clubs across the US.

Trump is one of the few cash-rich investors in the US who understands how to make money in golf. He was ready to exploit his more tactical luxury-branded golf business by picking up highly leveraged assets like Bedminster.

He has always recognized that golf clubs are incubator assets and that the underlying value of the land is an essential element to deal making. He has often said that money isn't made in the golf business; *"You make it in the real estate business.."*

Trump International Golf Club Los Angeles

Armed with cash, Trump found yet another worthy location in 2002 on the West coast. Recognizing a troubled course in southern Los Angeles' Ocean Trails, Trump began circling like a shark sensing blood in the water.

The 150-acre property was originally owned by developer Edward Zuckerman and a partner. The topography features a sloping terrain with sedimentary rock known for landslides. When Zuckerman developed Ocean Trails Golf Club, an 18-hole course designed by Pete Dye, he spent around $126 million hoping to double his investment over several years.

On June 2, 1999, a landslide unexpectedly sent the 18th hole crumbling into the Pacific Ocean along with half of the fairway and destroying three other holes effectively closing the course. The Ocean Trails Golf Club subsequently went into bankruptcy, and over two years later, Trump stepped in to restore the property. According to filings, Trump bought the club in late 2002, for $27 million.

Trump rebuilt the course, filling in the bunkers with granite and installing concrete below the surface. The 18th hole was as solid as Trump Tower. The facility included a 45,000 square foot clubhouse and additional residential lots that accommodate 75 houses.

Over the past few years, Trump sold off 18 lots at about 1.5 million each recouping much of the $30 million he spent to rebuild the course.

The club was renamed Trump International Golf Club Los Angeles, but it is located on the luxurious Palos Verdes Peninsula thirty minutes south of downtown Los Angeles. The club is known for views of the Pacific Ocean and Catalina Island and features three artificial waterfalls.

The landslide created an opportunity for Trump to purchase a trophy west coast golf club at an incredible discount. Many celebrities and high net worth investors regularly dine at the property and the *Michael Douglas Pro-Celebrity and Friends Golf Tournament* takes place there annually in April. As far as another catastrophic landslide, Trump believes,

"That land is solid. We checked carefully."

Trump National Golf Club Washington DC

In 2009, toward the middle of the last economic slump, Trump bought Lowe's Island Club from Chevy Chase Bank for $13 million extending his luxury golf empire. This was Trump's first acquisition in the Washington, DC region.

"As of late, [golf clubs] have made sense for us," said Eric Trump, Executive Vice President of development and acquisitions.

The 800-acre private golf club, renamed Trump National Golf Club Washington DC, contains two 18-hole golf courses. The Championship Course is a 72-par course designed by Tom Fazio and The River Course is another 72-par course added in 1999.

Since acquiring the club, Trump has invested over $10 million in a state of the art tennis center that features five indoor flexi cushion courts (10 mm rubber cushion to absorb impact) with wired cameras on every court. When the tennis center opened, Serena Williams was there to cut the ribbon and she said:

"This doesn't look like your average tennis facility, and I've been in a lot of tennis facilities. This one is the best one I've ever seen."

The course is undergoing substantial renovations in preparation for the upcoming 2017 Senior PGA Championship, one of the most prestigious tournaments in professional golf.

The Championship Course is the only course in Washington D.C., Maryland, and Virginia with large scale Potomac River frontage (over one mile) and each hole has been painstakingly built to take unprecedented advantage of the river's visibility and playability perspectives to challenge the golfers at all levels.

In 2015, six years after purchasing the club, Trump announced improvements totaling around $25 million. Members pay around $100,000 a year and monthly dues of about $700. Sources suggest that the club has roughly 1000 memberships including tennis and golf.

Trump National Golf Club-Hudson Valley and Trump National Philadelphia

As the recession rolled on, in December 2009, Trump acquired two more golf courses closer to home; The Branton Woods Golf Club in Hudson Valley and the Pine Hill Course in New Jersey purchased from Empire Golf.

Trump said in an interview with *The Real Deal*,

"These are great courses. I'm only buying the best. When they have capital behind them they will be really fantastic, and I'm buying them at good prices. And with that comes hundreds of acres of land, which I like having. These are phenomenal assets."

"These two courses are each considered among the finest in the country and I am proud to add them to my growing list of clubs." Trump said in a separate statement.

We could not verify the price point for these two clubs, but Trump said, "the two acquisitions would have cost $45 million each to build and take years for necessary approvals before construction could begin." The Branton Woods Golf Club in Hopewell Junction, NY was renamed Trump National Golf Club-Hudson Valley.

The 365-acre Pine Hill property overlooking downtown Philadelphia was renamed Trump National Golf Club Philadelphia. The original Pine Hill was designed by Tom Fazio, while Branton Woods was crafted by architect Eric Bergstol whose firm also developed and built the course. The golf course was built on the site of former Ski Mountain at Pine Hill in 1998.

Trump Goes on a Buying Spree

Trump picked up another bargain in August 2008 by acquiring the 4-year-old Shadow Isle Golf Club in Colts Neck for $28 million. New Jersey was the first state to have two Trump clubs. Trump said:

"I have the most successful club in New Jersey, the Bedminster club is amazing. I had no intention – and I looked at many clubs – the last thing I was looking for was a second course in New Jersey. It works with Bedminster because it's an hour away. It's not too close. But if I wasn't knocked out by this, in terms of potential – zero interest."

The 450-acre property includes a par-3 golf course and a 58,000 square foot clubhouse designed by Jerry Pate. In 2012, Trump continued digging for bargains and bought The Point Lake and Golf Club in Charlotte for $3 million renaming it the Trump National Golf Club Charlotte. He assumed liabilities to improve the Greg Norman-designed course, tennis courts, and facilities.

The purchase north of Charlotte was finalized after months of debate in the exclusive community along Lake Norman. Opponents worried the deal would raise home prices to an unaffordable level. In the end, Trump was successful in buying the club now boasting a dense community of 900 high-end homes.

Crescent Resources originally developed and built the community in the late 1990s. It has attracted NASCAR drivers, sports celebrities, medical professionals, and executives from the nearby Lowe's Company headquarters. The median house size is 4,500 to 5,000 square feet and the average lot size is one acre.

The club has an impressive village-style model including a tavern, general store, cobbler, meeting house, day care, and pro shop connected by a cobblestone road. We consider the Charlotte deal to be one of Trump's best acquisitions based on Return on Invested

Capital (ROIC). He paid $3 million and the club generates over $10 million a year in revenue. We value the club at $20 million, not a bad day's work for Trump.

Also in 2012, Trump found another deal in Jupiter. His third club in the state of Florida was the purchase of the former Ritz-Carlton Golf Club & Spa bringing the Trump Golf portfolio up to 14 properties worldwide. Trump thought the property fit well with his courses in Palm Beach and Doral.

"It's a great course, Jack Nicklaus did a fantastic job and it's got great membership, as well as a large acreage – 350 acres right in the middle of Jupiter," Trump said. "It's a spectacular property with a magnificent clubhouse and we're going to bring it to the next level."

The Jupiter property includes an 18-hole course and clubhouse, a full-service spa, and a fitness center encompassing approximately 75,000 square feet. According to filings, Jupiter generates over $12 million a year in revenue.

"I've had my eye on it since the first day I saw it," Trump said. "Nothing goes quickly."

Prior to acquiring Jupiter, Trump closed on the sale of the Doral club in Miami (Chapter 12) and began expanding his collection in Scotland (Chapter 13).

Valuing Donald Trump's Golf Collection

Given the substantial growth in Trump's golf portfolio, he began offering fee-based golf services for construction management and operations. He opened the Ferry Point course in the spring of 2015. The New York course worked out around $270 million to build and Trump negotiated a favorable 20-year lease to operate the club in which he should be handsomely rewarded. Trump did invest $10 million for the clubhouse and we suspect his return on equity will be above average given our run rate forecast ($5 million per year in green fees). Trump also has two new Dubai courses are expected to open by the end of 2017.

Trump International Golf Club Dubai (7,205 yards, par 71 course with a 30,000 square foot clubhouse) and Trump World Golf Club Dubai (designed by Tiger Woods) are both built by DAMAC Properties. This licensing deal extends Trump's footprint into the Middle East and further validates the strength of the luxury brand equity (discussed further in Chapter 16).

By increasing the number of clubs, Trump can offer purchasing benefits such as contracts for turf equipment, golf cars, and apparel. In addition, Trump has better purchasing power in the food and beverage category and his company can save up to 15 percent.

As explained in Chapter 10, valuing Donald Trump's golf courses is a tricky exercise because many of the clubs are considered trophy assets. We decided that the best method for valuing the golf portfolio is to breakout Doral and the European collection (Scotland and Ireland) in separate chapters (Chapters 12 and 13) and determine the value of the dozen other courses - owned and managed by Trump.

Our best estimate for income was derived from public filings and our own estimates. We believe that the dozen clubs (owned or managed by Trump) generate over $100 million of annual revenue. We have visited all of the clubs and we decided to score each property based on a number of attributes such as location, market visibility, demographics, and competition.

Our scorecard can be viewed below and as you can see we value the portfolio at $312 million. Keep in mind that Ferry Point and Dubia are managed. There is no debt on the Trump owned golf clubs other than the larger club at Doral and clubs in Europe.

In addition to generating strong cash flow, Trump has purposely diversified his investment portfolio into high-quality golf clubs. Including the larger clubs, Trump owns 15 properties that protect the billionaire from geographic concentration which includes the seasonality of weather. By not having all of his eggs in one basket, Trump has built a strategical investment portfolio that generates steady profits but also significant upside for redevelopment and licensing.

I assure you, Trump is not buying golf courses because he likes to play golf. He is acquiring the clubs to build his net worth and extend his branding blueprint. By dividing up his assets into multiple revenue streams the billionaire has amassed an enviable portfolio that offers scale advantages, resulting in wider profit margins.

More importantly, Trump's golf collection provides an important competitive advantage in which he can cross-market his real estate across multiple property sectors. Members of any of Trump's golf clubs can obtain reciprocal access to Trump-branded courses, as well as hotels and resort destinations. Similar to a Hilton Honor's Card or a Dividend Advantage Card, Trump is well-positioned to capture a global audience of customers that desire to live, eat, and play like Donald Trump. More on that in Chapter 16.

The Trump Factor

TRUMP GOLF			
Courses	Holes	Revenue ($mm)	Value ($mm)
West Palm	27	12.7	$38.1
Westchester	18	9.4	28.2
Bedminster	36	16.1	48.3
Los Angeles	18	13.0	39.0
Colts Creek	18	6.6	19.8
Washington, DC	36	14.0	42.0
Hudson Valley	18	4.2	8.4
Philadelphia	18	4.9	11.0
Charlotte	18	10.1	20.2
Jupiter	18	12.4	37.2
Ferry Point	18	1.0	10.0
Dubai	18	1.0	10.0
Total	261	105.4	$312.2
Trump Equity			$312.2

CHAPTER 12

DORAL: A DIAMOND IN THE ROUGH

"Doral is one of the most important golf properties in history and it is incredible to see the changes that the Trump Family has delivered in such a short period of time."
– Gary Player

The City of Doral in Miami-Dade County, Florida, occupies a land area of 15 square miles bordered on the west by the Ronald Reagan Turnpike, to the north the Town of Medley, to the east by the Palmetto Expressway, and to the south by the City of Sweetwater.

With a population around 100,000 people, Doral is known for its highly accessible transportation systems with proximity to the Miami International Airport. In addition to its commercial appeal, Doral is also known for its quality of life. The town has a large number of retail stores, banks, and restaurants that are just minutes away from South Beach.

In 1962, while Donald Trump was in high school at New York Military Academy, a well-known real estate developer by the name of Alfred Kaskel was snooping around south Florida to find his next big real estate deal. Kaskel, at the time, was around 63-years-old and in the prime of his successful real estate career.

Like Donald Trump, Kaskel launched his real estate career in New York City. Starting in the 1930s, he had built up around 17,000 apartments in Manhattan, Queens, and the Bronx. In the 1950s,

Kaskel was considerably wealthy and he began expanding his development business into central Florida, Boston, and Chicago.

In the late 1950s, he acquired 2,400 acres of swampland for around $49,000, intending to build a golf course and hotel. The massive south Florida development opened in 1962 and was named "Doral," an amalgamation of the first names of Kaskel and his wife, Doris.

While Doral is known for its more laid back lifestyle compared to South Beach, the town is best known for its rich golf history, in particular, the world famous Blue Monster golf course.

Back in 1960, Alfred Kaskel was said to be creating a "monster" in the middle of the swampy Doral community. When the course originally opened, it was known as the "Blue" course and the "Monster" name was tacked on because of the challenging amenities – swirling winds, water hazards, and tough layout.

When Kaskel opened Doral in 1962 it consisted of three golf courses – Blue, Red, and Par 3 - and the country club gained additional credibility when Arthur Ashe came on board as the tennis instructor in 1970. In 1987, a spa wing was added and the resort was renamed the Doral Golf Resort & Spa.

Like many snow birds, Fred Trump was a frequent guest of Doral Golf Resort & Spa. He would take his family down, usually at least once a year, to relax in the sunny south Florida setting.

From the day that Doral opened, the resort was known for its over-the-top amenities, but nothing trumped the prestige of golf. The Blue course was originally designed by Dick Wilson and it was home to Florida's very first PGA event in 1962. The famed Blue Monster course has hosted an annual PGA Tour event for 54 years.

In addition to Casper (who won the first Open Invitational in 1962), Jack Nicklaus, Lee Trevino, Hubert Green, and Ben Crenshaw have been champions at Doral. Raymond Floyd and Greg Norman each won three times.

The Blue Monster was converted into a World Golf Championship event in 1999 and, since that time, Doral has taken on more of a glitzy, corporate feel, with luxury suites eating up the prime viewing areas.

For many golf enthusiasts, Doral is considered the prime Florida warmup for the Masters in Augusta, another southern charm with a rich history of golfing legends.

The Blue Monster has lived up to its hype. In 2005 Tiger Woods beat Phil Mickelson in an 18th hole duel and Tiger defeated Lefty in 2006. Woods was quoted as saying,

"What Donald has done with this place is phenomenal. He does nothing half-way."

The purse has grown substantially over the years. The inaugural tournament won by Casper offered $50,000 total prize money in 1962 (still far more than most tournaments at the time) and today the coveted prize money boasts over $9 million. Prior to 2006, the tournament was dubbed the Doral Open and in 2007 it was renamed the Cadillac Championship. In 2016, the Blue Monster course became a World Golf Championship (or WGC) event and the tournament, held in early March, was then referred to as the WGC-Cadillac Championship.

Adam Scott took home the winner's share in 2016, around $1.61 million, in a field of 64 players from around the world.

In January 1994, KSL Recreation Corporation, an affiliate of Kohlberg Kravis Roberts acquired a majority interest in Doral Resort & Country Club for around $500 million. The transaction marked the third resort investment by KSL, following the purchases of PGA West and La Quinta Hotel Golf and Tennis Resort, both near Palm Springs. KSL was, at the time, one of the nation's largest owner/operators of "premier" golf facilities.

The new owners insisted that Doral needed to upgrade the resort so in 1997, after winning three tournaments at Doral, legendary golfer Raymond Floyd was commissioned to rejuvenate the Blue Monster. The course had suffered over three decades of wear and tear so Floyd was challenged to put some teeth in the monster by adding 18 new bunkers and lengthening the course by 186 yards. Jeff Babineau of *The Sentinel Staff* wrote:

"The rough will be grown so tough and gnarly it will draw comparisons to barbed wire."

Then in February 2004, around ten years after KSL's purchase of Doral, Real Estate Investment Trust CNL Hospitality Properties Inc. agreed to acquire KSL for $1.37 billion. Under terms of the deal, CNL agreed to assume $794 million in long-term debt in a move that would further extend the Orlando-based REIT's goal of becoming a leader in owning high-end destination resorts.

In addition to Doral, KSL owned luxury hotels, golf resorts and spas, including the Arizona Biltmore Resort & Spa in Phoenix and the Grand Wailea Resort & Spa on Maui in Hawaii. An affiliate of Deutsche Bank provided financing to CNL for a portion of the transaction.

Mired in massive leverage and expensive equity in the form of non-traded REIT equity (fees are generated by the REIT of around 15 percent on the cost of equity), the Doral deal had been restructured by CNL in 2007.

According to *Bloomberg*:

"Corporate debt (was) used to finance Morgan Stanley's 2007 acquisition of the hotel owner (CNL) near the peak of the real estate market." The restructuring was a complex deal in which debt was swapped out as equity and in 2011 Morgan Stanley was prepared to unload the highly leveraged real estate, including Doral."

Morgan Stanley had booked around $4.4 billion in real estate losses in 2008 and 2009. The other stake-holders, hedge fund manager John Paulson and Winthrop Realty Trust, Incorporated, were ready to unload Doral. It had been around fifteen years since the golf club had seen any capital improvements and the crippled country club was screaming for new life.

As a last resort, Paulson and Winthrop put Doral in Chapter 11 bankruptcy protection. The duo had foreclosed on five resorts and with $1 billion in senior debt and $525 million in mezzanine debt, the foreclosure allowed them to stall until an agreement could be reached with the mezzanine lender, MetLife. According to court filings, the owners of Doral believed that the value for all of the golf resorts "significantly" exceeded the $1.5 billion in debt that was owed.

Donald Trump was well aware of the troubles brewing in Doral. The billionaire had spent many summers playing golf as a child and his second home, Mar-a-Lago, in Palm Beach is an hour's drive from Doral. Trump recognized the value of the 800 acres and he knew that he was one of the few investors in the world who could bring the "Blue Monster" back from the ashes. Joe Passov with *Golf* Magazine said,

"The Blue Monster boasts one of the greatest makeovers in history."

It was perfect timing for Trump; he had 14 courses in his portfolio providing him with economies of scale in which he could leverage his human resources, as well as buying power, in which he could negotiate better deals with golf equipment and apparel chains.

More importantly, Trump had cash. Unlike many developers in 2011 who were still licking their wounds from the last recession, Trump was financially fit, armed with a modestly leveraged real estate portfolio and diverse streams of revenue from over 100 different operating entities.

Trump had experienced his financial failures in 2000 and he recognized that he could leverage his name without putting his growing fortune at risk. With corporate wealth shielded in hundreds of single purpose entities, Trump was no longer reliant on banks for doing deals, he was able to engineer his deals based on his #1 investment principle, the golden rule; he who has the gold, makes ALL the rules.

Trump had one other resource, and perhaps the most important as it relates to Doral; her name is Ivanka.

Trump's oldest daughter, Ivanka Trump, was pregnant when Doral went into bankruptcy. She was expecting her second child and as Senior VP at The Trump Organization, one of her primary responsibilities is negotiating acquisitions. Monte Burke with *Forbes* recounts:

"In the ninth month of her pregnancy, the sellers called to tell her they were accepting another, higher bid." Accordingly, Ivanka "thought the deal was dead."

A few months later she got a call from the lawyers and she learned, "The deal was back on." Ivanka had since delivered her daughter, Arabella, and she had to fly from New York to Miami to inspect the property. The newborn was just a week old, and as Ivanka explained, "I hated leaving her but I had to."

Trained by her dad as a shrewd negotiator, Ivanka stood firm with the cash offer to buy Doral, all 800 acres, for $150 million. Be careful what you ask for.

Donald Trump, who had played on the iconic golf course over 50 years ago, became the proud new owner of the Doral Golf Resort & Spa, or as he quickly renamed it, Trump National Doral Miami.

"This wasn't a discount price," Trump said in a telephone interview. "We're paying a very full price, especially in light of the fact of how much money we'll have to spend to bring it back to its original grandeur."

Trump acquired Doral in an entity referred to as Trump Endeavor 12 LLC and, according to records, Trump took out a loan in the amount of $106 million in 2012. Over the last three years the billionaire has invested in excess of $200 million in the property including new bunkers, longer fairways, and an assortment of challenging water hazards.

In August 2015, according to records, Trump took out a second mortgage on Doral in the amount of $19 million from Deutsche Bank, bringing his total debt on the club to $125 million.

Valuation

Doral is one of the most difficult properties to value because there are no close peers. The golf courses are all high-end and the iconic Blue Monster course is considered one of the best 18-hole courses in the world. The other challenge was that Doral operates a luxury hotel.

In order to provide an accurate value of the entire club we decided that we would use both the income approach and cost approach to valuation.

For the income approach we used the $100 million gross revenue figure disclosed in Trump's presidential filings. Extravagant hotels generate profit margins of around 20 to 30 percent, so we used 30 percent since we know Trump is an efficient operator and the asset deserves a premium multiplier.

Next we take the $30 million net operating income estimate and apply a cap rate. Ultra-extravagant resorts like Doral trade for a range of 6 percent to 7.5 percent. Recognizing that Trump has invested substantial capital in upgrades we decided that we would provide the club a premium "trophy" valuation, so we used 5.5 percent. In other words, we value Doral at $545 million using the income approach.

Now the best way for us to value Doral using the cost approach is to consider the recently closed sale of the White Course. According to our records, Lennar Homes and CC Homes paid a combined $96 million to acquire the 130-acre tract. The site was previously owned by a hotel company that filed Chapter 11 during the recession. The course was later deeded to GWC Miami property and controlled by the government of Singapore as a creditor in the bankruptcy case.

The price-per-acre of $738,000 is our best indicator of value as it relates to Doral because it is adjacent.

Recognizing that Trump has invested well over $200 million into the real estate, we can't ignore the potential of the income that the asset will generate over time. However, we also must recognize the value that Trump can unlock by developing the land at Doral into other mixed uses. For example: assume gambling gets legalized in Florida, Trump could roll the dice again (with low leverage this time).

The recent comp (White Course) provides us with a valuable clue. If Trump had just purchased Doral with no capital invested, his basis would be $187,000 per acre. Comparing that to the recent comp (White Course), Trump could have lined his pockets by $440 million – the difference between his land basis and the comparable sale.

In other words, we believe that Trump could develop a portion of the club and maintain a large percentage of his revenue stream (of $100 million). Assuming that he develops 30 percent of the club (mixed-use) we suspect there is another $177 million in value than can be gained. In summary, we value Doral at $722 million.

We view this as a conservative estimate; in five years the land costs for high-end residential in Miami could fetch $1 million per acre, equating to $240 million for Trump's upside (over the income being generated from the resort). Subtracting the debt of $125 million, we estimate Trump's equity in Doral at $597 million.

Recently the PGA decided to relocate the World Golf Championships-Cadillac Championship (since 2011) to Mexico where it will be called the World Golf Championships-Mexico Championship starting in 2017.

Only Augusta National, home of the Masters; Pebble Beach; and The Colonial in Fort Worth, Texas, have hosted tournaments for more consecutive years than the Blue Monster, the nickname for Trump National Doral's Blue course. This will not impact the profitability for Doral as it was more of a political ploy according to Trump:

"It is a sad day for Miami, the United States and the game of golf, to have the PGA Tour consider moving the World Golf Championships, which has been hosted in Miami for the last 55 years, to Mexico. No different than Nabisco, Carrier and so many other American companies, the PGA Tour has put profit ahead of thousands of American jobs, millions of dollars in revenue for

*local communities and charities and the enjoyment of hundreds of
thousands of fans who make the tournament an annual tradition.
This decision only further embodies the very reason I am running
for President of the United States."*

We suspect that Trump will use his branding power to forge other
corporate sponsors and leverage the ultra-extravagant property for
conferences and conventions. Arguably, Donald Trump ranks as one
of the most influential characters in golf and Doral is one of his blue
chip holdings. When *Golf.com* asked Trump what Doral means to him,
he replied:

*"It's meant beauty. It's meant competition. It's meant fun. I've met
wonderful people in golf. I just don't meet bad people in this game.
It's strange. I meet terrible people in real estate. I meet terrible
people in show business. I meet terrible people in politics. People
in golf are just incredible. And golf has allowed me to build some
great courses and save some great courses. I've created a lot of
jobs, a lot of happiness. So that's what it's meant. It's meant a lot."*

The Trump Factor

DORAL			
Items			Value
Resort			$545,000,000
Land Development			177,000,000
Total			722,000,000
Debt			(125,000,000)
Trump Equity			$597,000,000

CHAPTER 13

THE SCOTTISH DEAL MAKER

*"Everything I have done or attempted to do for Scotland
has always been for her benefit, never my own and I defy
anyone to prove otherwise."*
– Sean Connery

Donald Trump is the son of a Scotswoman by the name of Mary Ann MacLeod who emigrated from the Island of Lewis, off the coast of Scotland, to America where she met and married Fred Trump.

MacLeod was a common surname on the island then and is well represented in Scotland today. Mary Anne was born on May 10, 1912; her father was a fisherman named Malcolm MacLeod, and her mother was Mary Smith.

Mary Ann's grandfather was Donald Smith. He died in 1868 at the age of 34 when a squall overturned his boat while fishing off the Vatisker Point. Although Donald is a common name in Scotland, it's likely that Mary Ann named her son after her grandfather.

According to the Deutsche Welle website, the Island of Lewis has a strong local identity linked to the church. The island is arguably the United Kingdom's last religious stronghold. The Presbyterian faith is not as powerful as it was in Mary Anne's day, but until recently, the ferry did not sail on Sundays and many still observe the Sabbath.

According to Ellis Island records, Mary Anne left for New York aboard the Scottish-built *Transylvania* in 1930, at the age of 18. Mary's sisters had visited New York before her. When it was Mary's turn to make the trip, the teenager met 24-year-old Fred Trump, the son of a German immigrant who made some money running a hotel in the Yukon during the Alaskan gold rush. She regularly returned to Lewis before her death in New York in 2000 at the age of 88.

Mary Ann Trump died in New Hyde, New York and the notice in the *Stornoway Gazette* reads:

"Peacefully in New York on 7th August, Mary Ann Trump, aged 88 years. Daughter of the late Malcolm and Mary Macleod, 5 Tong. Much missed."

Trump's older sister, Maryanne Trump Barry, a senior judge, has visited Lewis dozens of times and is well liked there. According to *Deutsche Welle* website, last year she donated £160,000 (210,000 euros, $234,000) to a care home and hospice in Stornoway.

By following Donald Trump's roots back to Scotland, there is evidence to suggest that the billionaire's religious values were instilled by his mother. Donald Trump voiced:

"Advice from my mother, Mary MacLeod Trump: 'Trust in God and be true to yourself'."

Donald Trump was extremely close to his mother and his family-oriented values are largely attributed to his fondness for Mary Anne. In Trump's eyes, his mother was a courteous and highly respected member of the household and she was the foundation from which Trump learned to be polite. It would seem fitting that Donald Trump would one day honor his mother by bringing the art deal making back to his Scottish roots.

Of course, one of the most fascinating qualities of Scottish history is golf. The roots of the game go back to the 15th century. It seems that the Dutch may have actually invented the sport but the evolution of the game dates back to 1457 when King James II actually banned golf because the game was counterproductive to military training.

Today, Scotland boasts over 500 golf clubs and nearly 600 courses. According to leading sports writer, Jim Black is the *"most densely populated golfing real estate on the planet."* Scotland is recognized as the original home of golf and contains some of the finest golf courses, notably the Old Course, Carnoustie, Muirfield, Royal Troon and, of course, St. Andrews.

Trump International Golf Links and MacLeod House and Lodge

Since Donald Trump revealed his proposal in 2006 to create his exclusive golf resort in Scotland, complete with an eight-story five-star hotel, 950 timeshare apartments have sprung up along with a "Trump Boulevard" at the Menie estate, north of Aberdeen. The billionaire boasts of his Scottish roots stating:

"I think this land is special, I think Scotland is special, and I wanted to do something special for my mother," he told a press conference in Stornoway.

Trump's sister, Maryanne Trump Barry, exclaimed:

"My mother would be so proud to see Donald here today. She would be so proud to see what he's done... He's never forgotten where he comes from."

Trump began his Scottish quest when he bought a portion of the Menie Estate in Aberdeen with the intention of building a golf course and resort there. In 2006, Trump bought 800 acres from Tom Griffin, an American lawyer who made a fortune selling his legal expertise to the North Sea industry in the 1970s.

Later, Trump picked up another 600 acres bringing his total land assemblage to around 1,400 acres. The area is in northern Scotland and, although Aberdeen has far milder winter temperatures than one might expect; statistically it's the coldest city in the United Kingdom.

During the winter, especially through December, the length of the day is very short, averaging less than seven hours between sunrise and sunset at the winter solstice. It reaches a little over eight hours by the end of January, and by summer, the days are near 18 hours long.

Trump's golf club in Aberdeen was different from many of his more recent deals in the US; the Scotland project was completely sculpted from scratch. To develop the land in Scotland, Trump enlisted course architect Martin Hawtree, the man behind the Carnoustie Golf Links (home of the Open Championship in 2018).

One of Trump's biggest challenges with the land was the miles of protected sand dunes. Trump eventually won approval to construct the course even after local residents protested. Ultimately, Scottish officials decided the economic benefit outweighed the environmental degradation.

This Trump International property opened in 2012 despite painstaking efforts and ongoing drama from the announcement of the project's on March 31, 2006.

Painstaking Trials

On the Menie Estate, Trump renamed the 19-room house the MacLeod House and Lodge in honor of his mother.

The previous owner, Tom Griffin, had been re-acquiring parcels of land to re-assemble the estate and he paid a little more than $11 million for the bulk of it. He had developed golf courses in the past (Chapter 11) but he had never developed a site in what *Golf Digest* referred to as:

> "... *a mini-mountain range of coastal dunes, on linksland [that was] protected by a highly restrictive conservation designation.*

In the first pitch to the planning commission, Trump's application was turned down by one vote, but the Scottish government vetoed the group citing economic benefits. Trump won rights to build two golf courses, a clubhouse, a 45-room hotel, 950 vacation houses, and 500 residences.

Once Trump was able to obtain permission to build the golf community, the billionaire had to cross an even larger hurdle: to stop the Scottish government from erecting 11 offshore wind turbines in Aberdeen Bay, in clear view of Trump's recently acquired Menie Estate.

Trump did not want the wind turbines and was furious enough to lash out at Alex Salmond, the head of the Scottish government - a surprising target, because Salmond, the First Minister, was largely responsible for the approval of the planning application.

A Trump spokesman had accused Salmond of:

"... putting Scotland in dangerous territory by destroying some of its most pristine natural assets."

This was ironically the same argument that Trump's antagonists had been making against him. Another hurdle for Trump, in addition to the wind turbines and visibility concerns on the North Sea, were eyesores of several of the neighboring homeowners. Some alleged that Trump was trying to bully and intimidate the local landowners, forcing them to give up their land.

Most famous of these spats was Trump's battle with farmer and fisherman, Michael Forbes, who refused to sell Trump property and land in the middle of the Menie Estate where the course was being built. Trump once described Forbes' home as a "pigsty." At one point, the water to the home was shut off, but Trump's attorney, George Sorial, maintained it was an *"accidental consequence of construction work."*

Filmmaker, Anthony Baxter chronicled the conflicts and insults in his film, *"You've Been Trumped,"* which received critical acclaim globally.

Despite all of this controversy, Trump managed to open the course in July, 2012 with a huge media contingent present and Former Ryder Cup Captain Colin Montgomerie hailing it as a "marvel." The Scottish-born actor Sean Connery was named as the club's first member.

The golf media joined the cadre with many commentators agreeing that architect Martin Hawtree had created a landmark golf course. Before Trump Aberdeen opened, *Golf World* magazine announced that the course had gone straight into its UK course rankings at number eight, ahead of several British Open venues including Royal Lytham & St. Annes.

A First-Hand Account

When I arrived at Trump Aberdeen, I was prepared to witness one of Trump's all-time best deals. I had arranged in advance to test the Scottish countryside by taking in a few golf lessons and trips to the hometown driving range.

I arrived in Aberdeen by taxi in the pitch dark. As soon as I turned into the meandering driveway, I saw the MacLeod House lit up and I was eager to call it home for a few days.

After traveling by plane, train, and taxi to arrive at the destination, I was amazed at the beauty of Trump's spectacular property in the light of day. The Scottish property is one of the most breathtaking assets in his portfolio. I took plenty of pictures but they do not reveal the awesome natural beauty.

Trump had informed me in advance of the massive dunes, but he could not have managed to adequately explain the sheer immensity. The sun was shining and there were no clouds; the temperature was a perfect 60 degrees. The accommodations were exquisite and the staff at the MacLeod House was extraordinarily well-mannered.

In typical Trump-style, the billionaire hand-picks his staff and his CEO in charge of Aberdeen is Sarah Malone. She elaborated:

"Mr. Trump has invested millions in the renovation and restoration of a really important, historic building in the north-east of Scotland. It is right in the heart of our estate. We've built this entire service from scratch and we pride ourselves on hiring the best staff possible - those that have a natural aptitude for hospitality."

When the Scottish Open was hosted at Royal Aberdeen, the hotel welcomed world-class golfers including Justin Rose, Phil Mickelson, and Rory McIlroy. I stayed in the same room that Phil Mickelson had stayed in just weeks before my visit.

The interior of the MacLeod House bears some resemblance to Mar-a-Lago (chapter 9).

Vast rooms feature period pieces and bathrooms are decked out in Italian marble; the opulent property features a number of other fine amenities. A 'whiskey snug' is hidden in the basement with cozy armchairs in which to savor a wide selection of malts being offered – including Trump's own limited edition.

The restaurant and bar offer an extensive range of options, all highly praised, giving Macleod House top marks for food and beverages. Clearly, Donald Trump understands how to win over customers. Sarah Malone, CEO shared:

"We believe we have the best in Scotland on our doorsteps and it's all those little things that make the difference. It all adds up."

When I saw the land, I was overwhelmed by the imposing dunes and rugged Aberdeenshire coastline. It seemed a flawless site for a Trump International property. I have never seen such an unspoiled and dramatic seaside landscape; it is the perfect location for Trump's first development in Europe.

Trump plans to add a second course and, more recently, the billionaire has tabled plans for the course hoping to leverage his economic generators (jobs and taxes) in favor of satisfactory outcomes related to the wind turbines. Trump's master plan includes more golf holes in addition to lodging space, retail space, and residential uses.

According to sources, Trump has invested around 100 million British pounds (roughly $155 million US dollars) into the Aberdeen project. The potential for Aberdeen is strong, especially since Trump is gaining scale by acquiring multiple other clubs (one in Scotland and one in Ireland).

Given Trump's golf strategy of being a luxury golf course consolidator, I believe that it's most appropriate to analyze the value of scale and efficiency within Trump's expanding collection of trophy golf clubs. Let's move on to Turnberry . . . .

Trump Turnberry, Scotland

Trump's most recent acquisition in Scotland is the south Ayrshire link course known as Turnberry Golf Club. Many recognize the course for the legendary July match coined the "Duel in the Sun" in which Tom Watson and Jack Nicklaus battled toe-to-toe in a heated contest that ended with Watson's last-minute birdie on the 18th hole to claim victory.

More than a trophy golf club, Turnberry is an iconic masterpiece originally commissioned by Willie Fernie, a Troon Golf club professional, to design and lay out the championship 6,248-yard course. Work commenced in 1901, and by 1905, there were 260 members registered in the club.

Thanks to a railroad line that became the primary transportation hub through Ayrshire, the Turnberry Golf Club became a feature destination sparking the addition of a 100-room hotel and second golf course in 1909.

During World War I, Turnberry's golf course went into hibernation as the government converted the fairways to airfields for training pilots. The tremendous hotel was converted to a mess hall.

However, in 1921, the course roared back to life as peace resumed. It was then owned by a consortium of railroads that embarked on renovations and nearly two decades of golfing until 1941 when World War II forced Turnberry back into hibernation.

This time, the government faced arguments regarding its suitability as an airfield, but the popular vote lost and the government constructed a massive air base out of two-foot thick concrete and the hotel became a hospital. Many were convinced that Turnberry's time as a golf club was over.

However, after the war ended, the hotel ownership group (British Rail) decided to make an attempt to revive Turnberry. While remnants of the war efforts were noticeable, the majority of the ugliness was cosmetic. Turnberry's character remained and the undulating sand dunes fringing the seashore had been untouched.

Designer Mackenzie Ross is credited with restoring the Turnberry courses to their high quality. The Ailsa course was re-opened in 1951, a seaside links with stunning views of Ailsa Craig and the Isle of Arran.

In December 1997, Starwood Hotels & Resorts Worldwide, Incorporated, known for having some of the most distinctive brands in the hospitality industry, acquired the iconic Turnberry property for $51.5 million (SEC Filing 10K). Starwood was known for investing in upscale luxury resorts and the company had carved out a niche in marketing unique lifestyle brands.

Starwood owned and operated Turnberry over ten years under the Westin brand. In October 2008, Leisurecorp, Dubai World's sport and leisure subsidiary, purchased the Turnberry resort with Starwood continuing to manage operations under The Luxury Collection brand.

Starwood received approximately $100 million (US) for the deal and obtained a 50-year agreement to manage the hotel. The new owners decided to pump in another $49 million to restore the hotel. At the time of the announcement, Alan Rogers, Group-CEO, at *Leisurecorp* said:

> *"Turnberry is a significant addition to our property portfolio and we take seriously our responsibility of restoring the hotel and facilities to its former glory."*

Leisurecorp had already been operating in Dubai and across the world for several years identifying and acquiring sport, leisure, and lifestyle-related investments.

Then in April 2014, six years after Leisurecorp's acquisition, *The Independent* in London reported that Donald Trump paid Leisurecorp over $63 million (US) for his second Scottish golf club. Turnberry was the 17th golf property owned by Trump at that time, 12 of them in the United States. On the news, Trump told *golf.com*:

"I'm not going to touch a thing unless the Royal & Ancient ask for it or approve it. I have the greatest respect for the R&A and for (chief executive) Peter Dawson. I won't do anything to the golf course at all without their full stamp of approval."

Trump said he would invest *"many millions of dollars"* into the hotel and it would be the most luxurious in all of Europe when he was finished.

It's plain to see that Trump has doubled-down on Scotland. The Turnberry club has had a $300 million makeover and was able to host the Ricoh Women's British Open in 2015. Trump recently reopened the iconic course having already spent around $140 million to transform all of the golf holes. He intends to unveil a second 18-hole golf course in 2017 that should preserve Turnberry's legendary status as one of the best golf clubs in the world.

Several enhancements to the seaside gym include a change to the oceanfront par 4 ninth hole and a new par 3 that measures 235 yards and calls for a 200 yard carry from the championship tee. Trump's course's maximum length has been stretched to 7,450 yards. Par remains 70 and the renovated layout now includes three par-3s and three par-5s. Trump is hoping to land a British Open at Turnberry but it appears that the earliest slot for the prestigious event is 2022.

The most controversial change is the oceanfront par-4 ninth hole. Trump intends to convert it to a long par 3 to eliminate the hog's-back fairway and relocate the entire hole closer to the lighthouse. The new par-3 will measure 235 yards and calls for a 200-yard carry from the championship tees.

Trump International Golf Links, Ireland

A few months before Donald Trump announced the acquisition of his magnificent club in Turnberry, the billionaire was busy buying up yet another trophy in southwest Ireland.

On February 14, 2014, sixty days before Trump announced he was buying Turnberry, he publicized his first deal in Doonbeg, a luxury resort destination overlooking the Atlantic Ocean. Similar to Turnberry, the Doonbeg resort was also a distressed property in which the original developer was mired in debt.

Kiawah Partners was the master developer of Kiawah Island, a 10,000-acre barrier island located 21 miles south of Charleston, South Carolina. The company's subsidiaries included *Kiawah Island Real Estate*; *The Kiawah Island Club*, which encompasses The River Course designed by Tom Fazio, the Tom Watson-designed Cassique, The Beach Club by Robert A.M. Stern and Sasanqua, and the Members-only spa; *Freshfields Village*; and *Christophe Harbour* in St. Kitts, and *Doonbeg*.

Problems arose between the original owners, Kiawah Partners, cousins Charles "Buddy" Darby and Leonard Long, resulting in the sale of Doonbeg and the company's entire portfolio. The original developers invested more than €67m or $74,805,500 (US) in the Turnberry project.

When South Street Partners acquired the property, the company announced it would be "evaluating" their overseas holdings. In its 11 years of operation, Doonbeg Golf Club never recorded a profit. During its high season, the resort has a staff of 245 workers. The site has permits for an additional 61 holiday properties according to reports.

Doonbeg continued to sink into debt since opening its course in 2002 and lodge in 2006, but that did not deter potential buyers looking to cash in on the location and first-rate facilities. It sits in a key location in the golf-rich section of the Emerald Isle less than an hour's drive from the Shannon Airport and a half-hour's drive to another legendary links course at Lahinch and the Cliffs of Moher, a series of stunning 700-foot seaside bluffs.

The Doonbeg Golf Club is renamed Trump International Golf Links, Ireland, and the course is spread over 400-acres with 2.5 miles of frontage on the Atlantic Ocean and features an 18-hole championship golf links course. The world-renowned course is named the *"#1 Resort in Europe"* by *Condé Nast Traveler*, a *"World's Best"* and *"European Golf Resort of the Year"* by *Travel + Leisure*.

The Lodge at Doonbeg consists of 218 hotel suites, an expansive spa, and several restaurants all managed directly by the Trump Hotel Collection, Trump's award-winning hotel management company.

Greg Norman's company designed the golf course, and according to the golf legend's website, Doonbeg cost around $200 million which was more than expected and partly due to exchange-rate fluctuations. Trump was the perfect buyer. He had experience in the United Kingdom and knew how to operate luxury-branded hotels. Most importantly, Trump had cash.

How Much Is the European Collection Worth?

Trump's European golf portfolio is much harder to value. Aberdeen is a relatively new course and the number of golf memberships should increase as Trump continues to gain exposure throughout Scotland. The Turnberry acquisition was a tactical investment for Trump to add synergy to the two Scottish golf clubs providing greater brand awareness of the billionaire's growing golf businesses.

Based on our estimates, Trump has invested close to $500 million in the two Scottish clubs – Aberdeen and Turnberry – and the combined exposure should provide value for both European golfers but also U.S. golfers who are members of Trump's other clubs. Given the relevance of golf in Scotland, Trump has a tremendous competitive advantage in which he can market his European clubs to U.S. golfers enticing them to use all the courses in a reciprocal format.

In other words, Trump's European collection extends scale to his operation and that should allow him to increase overall golf revenue while also reducing costs due to economies of scale.

Trump has always viewed his golf investments as long-term assets where he derives the most value by developing or redeveloping the properties – always focusing on the highest and best overall uses.

In Aberdeen for example, Trump has land available for another 18-holes in addition to residential, retail, and hospitality components. The infrastructure is in place to accommodate a growing revenue stream that could ultimately produce comparable "resort like" valuations like Doral.

Also, Aberdeen's intrinsic development component has considerable potential if Trump sells excess land to a single family home developer and a hotel developer. Future development of 2,500 home sites at $80,000 to $60,000 per lot ($70,000 mid-point) X 1.32 exchange rate x 2,500 lots = $231 million in development proceeds. Also, a hotel parcel could fetch $5 to $10 million and retail shops could bring in another $10 million. It is possible Trump could unlock around $250 million in Aberdeen over the next decade.

Likewise, Turnberry recently reopened after Trump completed a $140 million overhaul. The future of this iconic club is similar to Doral in that it deserves a "resort" multiple and the "trophy" status makes the valuation more complex. Trump paid $63 million for Turnberry and we believe there is a symbiotic relationship as it relates to the acquisition and rehab costs. Why would Trump invest more in the rehab than the acquisition? Because it deserves a premium. We will use 20 percent, or $27 million, for Turnberry's value creation to date (there is obviously more value when Trump builds a second course).

Doonbeg, the last European acquisition, was the "feather in the hat" for Trump's golf portfolio. Similar to Doral and Bedminster, Trump smelled blood in the water and he was able to capitalize on the distressed situation by picking the Irish club up on the cheap. We know Trump paid much less than the developed cost (around $75 million). Again, Trump is no dummy when it comes to buying golf clubs and we consider $25 million a reasonable premium.

Obviously, Donald Trump is not going to provide us with his P&L statements for his European golf portfolio, and since we do not have EBITDA and building costs, we can only extrapolate the value using our limited resources. However, we consider our valuation of these assets in-line with other trophy golf clubs.

We're confident that Trump did not overpay and that he has re-framed from using high leverage. Also, given the fact that two of three clubs (Turnberry and Doonbeg) are somewhat established, we believe that there is ample revenue to service expenses on all three of the clubs. Therefore, we believe that Trump deserves $150 million (50 percent of our estimates) for his efforts related to consolidating three of the finest courses in Europe and providing a platform for members to enjoy the privileges of being a Trump golf member.

The Trump Factor

EUROPEAN GOLF PORTFOLIO			
Items			Value
Aberdeen (Scotland)			$125,000,000
Doonbeg (Ireland)			25,000,000
Turnberry (Scotland)			27,000,000
Total			
Trump Equity			$177,000,000

CHAPTER 14

THE TRUMP TOYS

"Private jets cost a lot of money."
– Donald Trump

Many billionaire investors own expensive toys that keep them entertained as they grow their fortunes. For some, it could be owning a professional sports team, and for others, it could be sailing around the world in a luxury yacht. Donald Trump had both.

Sports Franchise

Back in 1984, Trump owned the New Jersey Generals, previously a franchise of the United States Football League (USFL). He reportedly paid $9 million to become the owner of the Generals and, within a year, his team was one of the best in the league. Thanks in large part to Trump, the team landed television contracts with major networks like ABC and ESPN.

Although Trump bought the Generals as a hobby to get his mind off of real estate, he treated it as an investment hoping to earn a profit on his new franchising machine.

The USFL was a new concept and Trump anticipated becoming one of the early winners of the sports model that offered football fans real-time play, year-round. The key concept behind the USFL was for games to be played in the spring to avoid competing with the National Football League (NFL).

In the end, Trump knew that the two leagues would cannibalize one another and, after losing an antitrust lawsuit, he sold the franchise to Oklahoma oil magnate, J. Walter Duncan, just a year later. Many admired Trump's efforts to create competition for the NFL and the power of promotion that he brought to the sport.

However, this venture and the next few that followed would have Trump ultimately realizing that leveraging his name went much further when focusing on his circle of competence in real estate.

The Trump Princess Yacht

Trump also had another toy to entertain him and this one was more expensive. In 1988, he purchased a 282-foot yacht from the Sultan of Brunei, Adnan Khashoggi, for $29 million. According to *The Los Angeles Times*:

> *"The Trumps (then married to Ivana) did practically steal this third-largest motor yacht in the world. They snapped it up early this year for just $30 million, then spent $8.5 million on a 6-month facelift in the Netherlands."*

Trump renamed the vessel the *Trump Princess* and the lush new boat became a floating version of the *Lifestyles of the Rich and Famous*. Features included 11 double-sized staterooms (each named and decorated for a precious stone), 210 telephones, three elevators, a helicopter landing platform, a dance hall, a movie theater, a 15-foot swimming pool, and two 30-foot Monte Carlo speedboats.

In 1991, when Trump's financial empire started to unravel, he was forced to hand the keys back to the boat's lender. At that time, Trump had over $900 million in recourse (personally guaranteed) debt and the last thing that he needed was to boast about his "Ship of Jewels" (the subject of a chapter in Trump's book, *Surviving at the Top*) to the bankers holding the paper. Also, the boat cost Trump millions to operate and it became a drain for him financially.

In a 1991 *Reuters* story, Trump explained:

"I bought the boat in the high 20s. I sold the boat essentially for the mortgage that was on the boat. Forty to forty-two million, that was the amount of the loan that was on the boat."

The football franchise and 282-foot yacht were small bets for Trump compared to his other big wager, Trump Airlines.

Trump Airlines: Trump Shuttle

Also in 1988, when the billionaire was flying high, he took another crack at a new hobby that was outside of his circle of competence by purchasing Eastern Air Shuttle.

Unlike the unproven New Jersey Generals, Eastern was an established business with a record of 27 years of flights from Boston, New York City, and Washington, DC.

Trump paid around $365 million for the airline business but he had no cash invested. According to sources, he arranged to finance the business by taking out a corporate loan in the amount of $380 million from a consortium of 22 banks.

Trump's plan for the airline business was to convert the fleet of 17 Boeing 727s into a luxury shuttle service with many high-end amenities such as maple-wood interiors, chrome seat belt latches, and even gold-colored bathrooms. It was a big bet for the billionaire, especially since he did not anticipate the massive spike in jet fuel resulting from the first Iraq War.

With business slowing, fuel prices climbing, and the interest meter ticking, Trump decided to turn over the airline's Trump Shuttle, in 1992 after just four years. The operation of Trump Airlines officially ceased in April 1992, after it was rolled into the successor firm, Shuttle, Incorporated, later renamed US Air Shuttle. All that remains of Trump's airline ambitions seems to be his corporate fleet.

Lesson Learned: Focus On Your Circle of Competence

Although Trump's extensive toy collection – pro sports team, luxury yacht, and airplanes – don't appear on his financial statement today, the billionaire concedes that the financial setbacks were all rooted in one common thing: they weren't tied to real estate.

Trump doesn't like calling any of his setbacks "failures"; he prefers to label them "lessons."

Toys or not, Trump insists that all of them were investments and the reason that he no longer owns them is because they are not in his wheelhouse. By focusing on his core business of real estate, Trump has been able to increase his personal wealth dramatically without distractions. In the words of Kenny Rogers in *The Gambler*,

"You've got to know when to hold 'em, know when to fold 'em, know when to walk away, know when to run . . . ."

It really boils down to knowing when to cut the losses. The early 1990s were a pivotal period in Trump's life in which he knew he had to own his circle of competence and become a more disciplined investor. He knew that he could not successfully rebuild his net worth by participating in businesses that he did not understand or fully control.

Cutting losses on the football franchise, the ultra-luxurious yacht, and Trump Air was fairly easy for Trump because he recognized that the only way to increase wealth was to strip out the fat and build up muscle in his core real estate business. They were all bleeding and a Band-Aid fix would only delay the pain. Trump knew that by focusing on his core business he would eventually be able to rebuild his wealth and go toy shopping again.

Trump Air: Personal Fleet

Trump did manage to hang on to another big toy, a Boeing 727 that was built in 1969.

According to *The New York Times*, Trump paid around $8 million to buy the Boeing 727 from a financially troubled Texas company, Diamond Shamrock. In Trump's book, *The Art of the Deal*, he said a smaller Gulfstream jet would have cost more than twice as much.

"It was a little more plane than I needed," he wrote, " but I find it hard to resist a good deal when the opportunity presents itself."

Then in 2011, Trump upgraded the corporate jet to a Boeing 757. This plane was over 25 years old and was first delivered to Sterling Airlines (now a defunct Danish carrier) in May 1991. A few years later it was flying for Mexico's Transportes Aereos Ejecutivos S.A. (TAESA), now also defunct.

In 1995, the jet was purchased by Microsoft co-founder Paul Allen and for the next 15 years, the Boeing served as a corporate runabout for the billionaire's various interests. Trump purchased the plane from Allen to replace his Boeing 727.

The actual price for Trump's flying trophy is difficult to obtain. Some have valued it at $100 million and we know that he also spent vast sums on rebranding the aircraft with quite a few extravagant touches.

When he took delivery of the 20-year-old jet, he added amenities that are elaborate, "pimped-out" features about which we could only say, "Wow." The plane has 43 seats and all the fixtures are brushed with 24-karat gold. There are several common areas including a dining room, VIP seats, and the main lounge with a 57-inch television and state-of-the-art sound system. If you don't want to watch TV with everyone else, each individual seat also comes with its own personal entertainment system.

Trump's bedroom has a queen-size bed, gold silk on the walls, and pillows decorated with the Trump family crest. The master bath has a shower and a 24-karat gold-plated sink ... of course. All of the toilet seats are re-upholstered with Edelman leather.

In addition to the 757, Trump has four other registered aircraft: three Sikorsky helicopters, a fleet that has become a critical part of the billionaire's image he has sought to project on the campaign trail, and a 19-year-old Cessna 750 Citation X – the only one of the five without the Trump name painted on it in large letters.

> *"Everything that they did on it is very, very, spectacular," John Dunkin, Trump's pilot told the Smithsonian Channel's Mighty Planes. "It's very fast airplane for a large airplane. It's extremely comfortable. It takes turbulence very well. It's kind of like the Ferrari in the airline category airplane."*

According to Boeing, the 757 has a top speed of 609 miles an hour and can fly up to 4,400 miles without stopping. Trump and his management team take frequent flights to visit his golf clubs in Scotland and the 757 serves as a perfect method of transportation for the 3,200-mile trip.

The Boeing has Trump's surname emblazoned in big letters on the outside and gold-plated fixtures inside. In a documentary, Donald Trump described:

> *"The plane is very much an extension of the Trump brand."*

According to *The New York Times* regarding the Cessna:

> *"The Cessna (seats 12) has flown more than the other airplanes and is worth around $15.3 million new."*

Our sources suggest that the Cesna is worth around $3 million today. Trump recently upgraded one of his personal choppers to a Sikorsky S-76, the manufacturer's top-of-the-line for private aviation. It was even featured in CNBC's *"Super Lives of the Super Rich"* in a segment entitled *"Pimp My Chopper."*

To make the interior luxury-ready, Trump hired Eric Roth, the famed aircraft interior designer based in Long Island, New York. To redo the interior, Trump probably spent at least another $750,000.

The whole interior is outfitted with 24-karat gold-plated hardware — from the seatbelts to the handles. Trump also had his family crest painted on the side, in gold, of course. The shelves of the Trump chopper were stocked with water – Trump Ice spring water.

"If it's got the Trump name on it, it's got to be the best of the best," Roth said. *"And this helicopter is worthy of his name."*

We estimate that Trump's three helicopters – two 1989 Sikorsky S-76Bs and one 1990 Sikorsky S-76B – are worth around $4 million combined.

Prior to Trump's presidential announcement, he used the fleet of aircraft for business, mostly to help shuttle key employees to job sites across the globe. With a growing pipeline of golf clubs and hotels, The Trump Organization has become a worldwide real estate investor and licensee and the 757 serves as an efficient method of transportation.

Although Trump does not have debt on the aircraft assets, the costs of maintaining them are considerable. Flying the 757 costs nearly $5,000 an hour in fuel alone. Chartering a 757-200 costs $15,000 an hour.

Also, Trump pays hanger fees, taxes, and pilots. We estimate that it costs Trump over $1 million annually to operate the fleet, excluding fuel.

That's not cheap. However, Trump's businesses generate substantial cash flow and like most developers, he charges his businesses for use of the plane so the fleet serves as more than an expensive toy collection, it is an investment. Trump explains:

"But it [the use of planes] can be an absolutely vital tool for business."

For example, Trump uses one of his Sikorsky S-76B's in Scotland to shuttle customers across the United Kingdom. It was shipped to Scotland in 2015, for the use of clients of Trump Turnberry Resort in Scotland.

"The sky's the limit at Trump Turnberry, with exclusive helicopter charter now available for guests for quick and seamless travel to destinations across Scotland and beyond," the resort's website reads.

In total, we value Trump's fleet of aircraft at $107 million. Although the aging fleet does not represent a significant portion of the billionaire's worth, the real value in the toy collection is in the marketing potential and luxurious status that the fleet represents. In other words, Trump's fleet serves as flying billboards suggesting *"I am worth billions."*

Trump has several other toys that we consider essential to the billionaire's treasure chest. As noted above, Trump made the pivot in the early 90s away from non-core assets to real estate and began to focus on his circle of competence and investing in land once again.

Trump Winery, Charlottesville, Virginia

In 1989, John Kluge was named the richest person in America by *Forbes*, worth an estimated $5.2 billion. The media mogul made his fortune by selling TV stations that became the nucleus of News Corporation's Fox Network. Educated at Columbia Business School, Kluge was known to be a shrewd deal-maker with a passion for luxury. He once owned a Scottish castle, a 200-foot yacht, and a 10,000-acre estate in Virginia called the Albemarle House.

Kluge was married to former Patricia Rose Gay, once a model who became well-known in social circles. In 1990, the two split in what the press referred to as "irreconcilable differences" and, as part of the settlement, Ms. Kluge kept a 45-room mansion in Charlottesville, Virginia and a shooting lodge in the Scottish Highlands.

Dubbed by *Forbes* as a "cheapskate billionaire," Mr. Kluge boasted he would leave his hat and coat in his car to avoid tipping at a restaurant coat check; however, Ms. Kluge was known as a spender who loved to indulge in the finest of things, including the wine business.

Ms. Kluge spent millions of dollars on the Charlottesville property investing heavily in the 23,000 square foot home containing eight bedrooms, 13 bathrooms, and private chapel, all part of a winery operation. By 2008, she had racked up an enormous debt with over $65 million invested in the Charlottesville winery, yet when the recession hit, the banks called the loans.

The lenders forced her to sell most of her assets, including jewelry and home furnishings (a Chippendale dressing commode that sold for $338,500 and a Qing Dynasty table clock that fetched $3.8 million). All told, *Forbes* reported the 933 items brought in $15.1 million but she was unable to stave off the long list of creditors.

Ms. Kluge filed for bankruptcy and proceeded to hire Sotheby's International Realty to market the estate for $100 million. It did not sell. Later, the price was cut to $48 million and, in early 2010, the price was slashed to $24 million. Eventually, the banks got testy and decided to foreclose.

In early 2011, Donald Trump, who knew both John and Patricia Kluge, decided to fly his chopper down to Charlottesville. It was not a sightseeing trip for the billionaire; he was there for one thing, he smelled blood in the water.

Upon first examination, Trump could see that the loans on Kluge's estate were highly leveraged and he would need to put together a tactical blueprint to cash in. First he decided to acquire the winery that was pledged to three big lenders for around $40 million. The opening bid for the vineyard was $19 million and no buyer stepped in. To squeeze the bank, Trump was able to buy the 260-acre front lawn first.

That was part of Trump's plan. He knew that if he could buy the land in front of the 45-room mansion, nobody else would buy it and he would ultimately get what he wanted. It goes back to Trump's favorite golden rule of investing: *"He who has the gold makes ALL of the rules."*

Trump paid just $150,000 for the front lawn and waited patiently for the next acquisition when, a couple of months later, the Kluge vineyard hit the auction block. Trump swooped back in and snapped it up for $6.2 million, outbidding Virginia developer Sal Cangiano.

By then, Trump had acquired the vast majority of the land surrounding Albemarle House. He knew that he had been victorious in putting the mansion's lender, Bank of America, into checkmate. It was virtually impossible for a future buyer of the mansion to drive into or out of the house. Eric Trump recounts:

"It was a 1,500-acre sea of Trump. We surrounded them. Even the road that went to the house was on our property."

At the time of the auction of the mansion, Trump owned the vineyard, winery, and much of the land around the house purchased for a portion of their actual value nearly a year prior. He wound up paying $6.2 million plus an additional $1.7 million for equipment and inventory, far less than the $60 million the business and property had been valued at by the banks.

Bank of America wanted $22.8 million for the house, but after Trump was able to outfox the bank - his investment was a small fraction, according to Eric Trump. In Chapter 2, we explained that Trump had acquired Mar-a-Lago in a similar way. He bought the beach and threatened to build the "ugliest building ever" in order to obstruct the neighboring views. That is how he was able to pick up the south Florida mansion at a bargain price.

Trump used the same strategy in Charlottesville. He was able to negotiate an incredible deal by flexing financial muscle, exhibiting patience, and most importantly, using a tactical blueprint that forced the bank into taking "peanuts" (as Eric Trump said). At the end of the day, Trump was able to buy the house for $6.5 million and the collective estate for under $13 million, proving that he had pivoted into a much more powerful negotiator.

Today, Trump operates a winery on the property and I visited the 1,300-acre site when the company was bottling wine. There are nearly 200 acres of French Vinifera grape varieties, and Trump Winery is Virginia's largest vineyard and the largest Vinifera vineyard on the east coast. The winery features over 50,000 square feet of state of the art winemaking facilities, a 100,000-gallon tank capacity, and a 750-barrel cave producing sparkling, white, and red wines. The property also boasts wedding and convention space.

Since visiting the property in Charlottesville, Trump has since opened up the mansion as a bed and breakfast with 10 bedrooms including a luxurious log cabin that John Kluge once called his "thinking room."

The rooms, which range in price from $399 to $699 for one night and one person, include a fully stocked gourmet mini-bar and a marble-finished bathroom with Trump Spa Bath Collection amenities. Meticulously manicured English-style gardens surround the estate.

"It's palatial," Tricia Traugott, the author of local wine blog Charlottesville Uncorked says about the space. "This is like something you'd see in Bavaria at one of King Ludwig's castles."

Trump has suggested in the past that the company may build a golf course on the land and that could enhance the value of the Charlottesville estate. The University of Virginia would be a major traffic generator for the golf club and other nearby attractions including Thomas Jefferson's Monticello, James Monroe's Ash Lawn-Highland, and numerous Virginia wineries.

We value Trump's Charlottesville property at $50 million. The property has no debt on record.

Other Trump Mansions

In 1996, Trump purchased a 213-acre property in Bedford, NY called Seven Springs. Trump told *The New York Times* he had planned to use the 39,000-square-foot stone and glass mansion as a suburban home for himself, Melania, and their son Barron.

Trump reportedly paid $7.5 million for the property. He originally planned to use it as a golf course but faced strong opposition from the locals who were concerned about chemical run-off from the course going into a nearby lake.

Seven Springs was built in 1919 (according to our sources) by *Washington Post* owner Eugene Meyer (the father of publisher,

Katherine Graham) and its value now is about three times more than the original purchase price paid by Trump.

In the last two decades, Trump has spent much of his time during the summer months at Seven Springs. The main house is anchored by a 50,000 square-foot mansion with 60 rooms, 15 bedrooms, and two servants' quarters. The estate also has three pools, including an indoor pool.

In total, Trump has amassed a personal toy collection of around $180 million. As part of the billionaire's blueprint, the dealmaker has maintained a more focused strategy of only investing in assets that he firmly understands and are relevant to his blueprint. His small wager in the sports and airlines business served as a valuable lesson leading him back to circle of competence. By leveraging his passion for property and his savvy deal-making skills, Donald Trump is not likely to hit too many other balls into the rough. He has become a more mature investor waging only where he knows the odds of winning are the best.

The Trump Factor

TRUMP TOYS			
Items			Totals
Boeing 757			$100,000,000
Helicopters			4,000,000
Citation X			3,000,000
Charlottesville, VA			50,000,000
Seven Springs			23,000,000
Totals			92,500,000
Trump Equity			$180,000,000

CHAPTER 15

A BLUEPRINT WORTH BILLIONS

*"If you want to succeed you should strike out on new paths, rather
than travel the worn paths of accepted success."*
- John D. Rockefeller

John D. Rockefeller was co-founder of Standard Oil and he became
the world's richest man and the first American to be worth more
than a billion dollars when he controlled 90 percent of all oil in the
United States at his peak.

Rockefeller died in 1937 and since that time (79 years ago) the
number of billionaires in the United States has grown to 1,694.

Donald Trump says he's worth around $11 billion and that includes
over $1 billion in cash and marketable securities. His presidential
filings indicate that the billionaire has 14 entities with bank debt in
which he owes around $315 million.

As mentioned in Chapter 1, at one-point, Trump was responsible
for nearly $900 million personally before he made the pivot from
a speculator to an intelligent investor. The failures in Trump's
businesses have been consistently overshadowed by his successes,
although you may not realize that based on media coverage of Trump.

Similarly, Rockefeller's enormous wealth and success made him
a target of mudslinging journalists who viewed him as a symbol of
corporate greed and criticized the methods with which he built his
empire. As *The New York Times* reported in 1937:

"He was accused of crushing out competition, getting rich on rebates from railroads, bribing men to spy on competing companies, of making secret agreements, of coercing rivals to join the Standard Oil Company under threat of being forced out of business, building up enormous fortunes on the ruins of other men, and so on."

Rockefeller and Trump both generated large sums of wealth but the road to success was not paved in gold. There were bumps along the way and for Trump there were a few dead ends. In the book, *If You Must Speculate, Learn The Rules*, Frank Williams wrote:

"If you are intelligent, the market will teach you caution and fortitude, sharpen your wits, and reduce your pride. If you are foolish and refuse to learn a lesson, it will ridicule you, laugh you to scorn, break you, and toss you to the rubbish-heap."

Suffering through adversity can be devastating, but it's because of Trump's financial failures that he has evolved into a disciplined investor who understands that monetary success encompasses playing good offense (i.e. earning money) and defense (i.e. spending as little as possible). This parallels another billionaire, Warren Buffett, who also witnessed near financial failure when he was a child.

Many of you may not know that Buffett – now worth $66.4 according to *Forbes* – was not born rich. Long before his prized conglomerate, Berkshire Hathaway, achieved iconic success, the billionaire struggled to keep the first asset, a New England textile mill afloat. In the 1960's many textile mills were moving south (due to cheap labor and raw materials) and after pouring money into Berkshire Hathaway and later trying to sell it, the plant eventually shut down.

Buffett had already begun to diversify so obviously Berkshire Hathaway was able to turn a failure into a success, yet it was through failure that Buffett was able to learn and ultimately succeed. In his biography, The Snowball, he put it this way:

"You walk down the street and you see a cigar butt, and it's kind of soggy and disgusting and repels you, but it's free ... and there may be one puff left in it. Berkshire didn't have any more puffs. So all you had was a soggy cigar butt in your mouth. That was Berkshire Hathaway in 1965. I had a lot of money tied up in the cigar butt ... I would have been better off if I'd never heard of Berkshire Hathaway."

Buffett's firsthand brush with failure during his early years strengthened two defining traits that would shape the rest of his life; a fierce determination to attain financial success and the kind of strong appreciation for value that only those who have experienced the pain of failure can understand fully.

Failure is a humbling exercise, especially for billionaire investors, but I am certain that every billionaire investor has experienced failure that ultimately became the driving factor for their successes.

Trump's defining moments would be in his later years, but like Buffett, the two billionaire investors became branded by their combined discipline and value-seeking traits. Through the failures, they witnessed transformative effects that served to be their defining moments and the mark of superiority all driven by their "extreme conservatism" habits.

Warren Buffett used "extreme conservatism" to create an enormous competitive advantage, as he explained:

"The years of poverty since Father's death had touched me only lightly. They had developed in my character a serious concern for money, a willingness to work hard for small sums, and an extreme conservatism in all my spending habits."

Donald Trump learned over the years, especially after witnessing failures, that being greedy and disciplined could allow him to negotiate shrewd deals like no other. He had to learn from is failures first, and such a risk-averse outlook allowed him to take advantage of the period preceding the financial tsunami referred to now as the Great Recession, where he was able to triple his net worth.

Trump became tough and it was through his failures in business that he learned to become a disciplined investor, as Sir John Templeton once said:

> *"To buy when others are despondently selling and sell when others are greedily buying requires the greatest fortitude and pays the greatest ultimate rewards."*

Trump became battle-tested. His failures taught him the meaning of risk and the most powerful words in the investing world: *Protect Your Principal at All Costs.*

In a *Wall Street Journal* article Anthony Scaramucci wrote:

> *"He (Trump) has demonstrated an ability to take punches and get off the mat while others without his fortitude and ingenuity would have crumbled."*

As a real estate developer and now financial analyst I have great respect for Donald Trump. It takes enormous courage and perseverance to pick up the pieces when you're down and then to rebuild the nest egg – one straw at a time. Scaramucci explained:

> *"Most of his critics have never dared to step into the entrepreneurial arena where there exists the potential of embarrassing defeat."*

Not Donald Trump. In the previous chapters I have provided you with a detailed blueprint of Trump's successful transformation from a real estate builder into a world-class developer, businessman, and entrepreneur. As I explained in Chapter 1, investing is a process in which we all make mistakes and ultimately the secret formula for success is summed in the word *discipline.*

What separates Trump from many investors however is his vision. I decided to title my book *The Trump Factor* because it is much more than just a book about Donald Trump's real estate empire. *The Trump Factor* is the mark of success and, while the Trump name embodies the characteristics of quality and value, it also signifies strength, determination, wisdom, humility, and patience – all attributes that are learned through discipline. What makes *The Trump Factor* unique?

Certain real estate projects rise above the rest to become true "trophy class" assets. Many such as the Empire State Building, the General Motors Building, the Chrysler Building, and others are well known. When these properties reach trophy status, their value is based on a different dynamic than simply cash flow and cap rates. Inherent in these assets is the notoriety that they've achieved plus their rarity.

More modest projects are called Class A or Class B and some are even known as "commodity" buildings - those that certainly do a good job at providing office space or residences but don't have any special cachet or significance.

A developer may not set out to build a "trophy" building – although, in fact, some do plan to design and develop an asset worthy of the designation. Donald Trump is a developer who has designed and developed Trophy Class buildings throughout his entire 40-year career.

Most developers are the "quarterbacks" of a team assembled to develop a property. They push very hard for every aspect of the project to be successful from the acquisition of the land site to the appropriate rezoning of the site.

Through it all, legions of professionals are necessary – and Trump assembles teams that are comprised of the BEST of the BEST. Simultaneously, the architects must be interviewed and their proposed designs must be reviewed and vetted by yet another team of highly qualified architects and engineers, many of whom work directly for the Trump Organization.

This level of energy and attention to detail continues through each step of the never-ending process. From the ceiling heights to the chandeliers and sconces used to light the interior, each are selected with great effort and understanding of the image that is being presented to the "client." This client may be a hotel guest, a condominium purchaser, or an office tenant. Great pride is also a characteristic necessary to successfully meld these components together.

Say what one will about the Presidential aspirations of Donald J. Trump and his campaign strategies to become our next Commander in Chief. However, no one can doubt, dismiss or "diminish" his development acumen. His properties withstand the test of time both physically and in design. He can walk through a project that he built 20 years ago and point out how certain decisions were made regarding carpet color and door design. This is a rare breed of developer whose talent is born, not made.

The Numbers Don't Lie

According to the *Bloomberg Billionaire Index*, Donald Trump is worth $3 billion, just $100 million higher than reported a year ago. *Forbes'* latest estimate was $4.5 billion and *Fortune* weighed the billionaire in at $3.9 billion.

Before providing you with my consolidated estimate of Trump's net worth, let me remind you that I have examined each and every property owned by Trump and I have also assembled a team of analysts and experts who have assisted me over the course of three years. To be perfectly clear, this book was not written to be a puff piece for Donald Trump to boast about his fortunes.

My job is to provide you with one simple thing: the facts. Hopefully, this research serves as a useful and reliable indication of Donald Trump's true net worth with a well-documented blueprint of each and every asset.

Trump's Liquid Assets

Obviously, Trump did not provide me with a copy of his bank accounts so I had to construct a model based on public filings and other reliable sources. *Forbes, Fortune*, and *Bloomberg* have all previously suggested that Trump's liquid securities are valued at around $300 million. The presidential filings provide a snapshot of the securities portfolio but we have no knowledge of Trump's percentage of ownership for each stock in the portfolio.

Also, most people forget that Trump's real estate generates substantial cash flow after debt service. That should serve as a good benchmark for to develop an accurate accounting of Trump's liquid assets.

As discussed in previous chapters, Trump owns several large *cash cows* that throw off chunkier income as well as a diversified portfolio of smaller deals that produce steady income with less geographically concentrated risk. Obviously, Trump has most of his net worth tied up in real estate, but the assets generate a steady cash flow with which to reinvest into securities or make new investments (or fund a political campaign).

After reviewing the *cash cows* such as Trump Tower (Chapter 2), 40 Wall (Chapter 3), Vornado Deals (Chapter 4), Chicago (Chapter 6), and Doral (Chapter 12), we believe that the billionaire rakes in around $500 million a year. This does not include the licensing deals that generate development fees, sales commissions, or management revenue. We are not including the licensing revenue in our cash flow model since we include it in the brand chapter.

In addition, Trump has a steady stream of book royalty checks that we estimate could bring in close to $1 million per year. Most well-known authors also benefit from high-profile speaking engagements and that was the case in 2014 when Trump was paid $1.4 million for four speeches.

Our total estimate for Trump's annual cash flow is $550 million, pre-tax. This breaks down by categorizing the larger deals at $500 million a year, the smaller deals at $45 million, and additional revenue generated by books and speaking engagements at $5 million a year.

Using the $300 million starting point indicated by *Forbes*, *Fortune*, and *Bloomberg*, and estimating that Trump's after tax cash flow is around $300 million a year as well, our combined cash and securities estimate is $600 million. In addition, Trump was able to refinance a number of properties including Trump Tower, 1290 Avenue of the Americas and Trump Las Vegas, where he pocketed around $320 million - our estimate - and we believe he generated at least $150 million from condominium sales from the Chicago property since it opened.

Finally, we believe that Trump's liquid assets are much more than $300 million and quite possibly could be in excess of $1 billion. He loaned his campaign $50 million in June so we deduct that from our model estimate of $1.070 billion to arrive at a cash and liquid securities estimate of $1.020 billion.

Trump has an estimated $630 million in debt, according to *Bloomberg*, that includes $170 million advanced by Deutsche Bank to redevelop the Old Post Office in Washington, DC. Given the fact that Trump's brick and mortar assets are worth over $5 billion and he has roughly $1 billion in liquidity - $6 billion total, we consider Trump's 10.5 percent loan-to-value ratio to be conservative.

Trump has ample liquidity in the form of cash on hand and cash flow from real estate in order to pay off all of his debt if needed. Most publicly-traded REITs have around 30 percent to 40 percent leverage and Trump's balance sheet is well-positioned for any sudden spike in rates or modest recession.

In summary, we estimate that Donald Trump's global real estate empire is valued at $5.046 billion after debt. This estimate is more than a WAG (wild ass guess) as we have conducted extensive research to arrive at our conclusions. The facts suggest that Donald Trump has become a much more disciplined investor over the years and his most recent deals - The Old Post Office and Doral - validate the point that he has become an institutional player competing with assets that deserve "trophy" premiums.

Pick four buildings in a major market that would be valued similarly (i.e. 4.5% cap rate) and there will be a Trump building on the list. Remember, a trophy will generate the highest number of bidders, have the final 2 or 3 bidding aggressively, and will trade at a price higher than anticipated due to the trophy nature of the asset.

This is an important point since many investors - Middle East, Chinese, etc.- only want to own iconic, trophy assets. That's where

Trump's properties have a big competitive edge and why there is true power in *The Trump Factor*!

We believe the intrinsic value of Donald Trump's vast real estate empire including cash and marketable securities is $6.066 billion, almost double the amount reported by *Bloomberg* and *Fortune*. We believe the discrepancy is largely due to the fact that the other media organizations have not considered all of the holdings and that journalists have not utilized valuation metrics comparable to trophy-like properties. We have opted to take a more granular assessment of the entire portfolio hoping to arrive at a more accurate calculation of Donald Trump's net worth.

The Trump Factor

Trump Property	Totals
TRUMP FACTOR SCORECARD	
Trump Vegas	$48,850,000
Scotland/ Ireland	177,000,000
Trump Toys	180,000,000
Trump DC	222,254,870
Trump Chicago	264,000,000
Mar-a-Lago	300,000,000
Trump Golf	312,000,000
Other (NYC)	330,000,000
40 Wall Street	400,000,000
Doral	408,000,000
Trump Hotels	814,000,000
Trump Tower	993,000,000
Cash/Securities	1,020,000,000
Total	$6,066,104,870
Trump Equity	$6,066,104,870

CHAPTER 16

FOLLOW THE YELLOW BRICK ROAD

"Oh no, my dear; I'm really a very good man;
but I'm a very bad Wizard, I must admit."
- The Wizard of Oz

In the Introduction I told you that I was going to take you on a journey to expose the Wonderful Wizard of Trump. By peeling back the curtain of Donald Trump's vast financial empire, I was hoping to provide you with a deep dive into the many real estate holdings and related assets owned by the billionaire from Brooklyn.

We have now completed the journey that took me over three years and I am now ready to reveal to you one of the most misunderstood secrets.

There is little doubt that Donald Trump is worth an estimated $6.06 billion based on tangible intrinsic value; however, I am now going to reveal to the world the combined *net worth* of Donald Trump based on his *tangible* and *intangible net worth*.

The value of the Trump brand has been estimated at $3.3 billion by Donald Trump. This number has not been pulled from thin air, as some have suggested. The respected consulting group *Predictiv* placed a $3 billion valuation on the Trump brand in 2011. The $3.3 billion figure reflects some added compounded growth since then.

When *Bloomberg Businessweek* attempted to calculate Trump's net worth in July, 2016, the magazine took a very limited view of Trump's brand value, and estimated its worth at a mere $35 million. This number was just a plain-vanilla projection based on Trump's annual revenue from ongoing brand licensing deals. "Was it an attempt to create a story by using elementary valuation techniques to devalue Trump's holdings?" That is up to you to decide.

This chasm in valuations, between $3.3 billion and $35 million, illustrates how easy it is to overlook the earnings power of the Trump name. The reason is not necessarily media bias. It's just that evaluating the Trump brand on typical multiples-of-revenue terms is a pointless exercise because there is nothing typical about the Trump brand. You could no more use this elementary valuation on the Louis Vuitton brand, Apple brand or Google brand. Ten years ago Google had negative earnings - how could the company be worth billions with a negative EBIDTA? I don't know what year they started earning a profit, but they were negative for years.

The Trump brand, simply put, is *sui generis*. There is no other brand like it in the world. When you look more closely at the reasons why, you can understand how the value of the brand is defined by the staggering cost of building from scratch a brand of equal scope and power.

There are three essential characteristics of the Trump brand that make the brand truly extraordinary. Taken together, they make the Trump brand a one-of-a-kind phenomenon. While many other brands may share one or two of these attributes, there is no brand in the world that shares all three.

1. Trump is a luxury brand, but unlike most other luxury brands, the Trump brand has an unapologetic Alpha Male character. Few, if any, luxury brands stand so unabashedly for values such as confidence, dominance, strength, bravery and non-conformity – all highly valued traits among luxury buyers.

2. Trump is an iconic brand, but unlike most other iconic brands (Apple, Nike, Coca-Cola), the Trump brand is privately owned and operated by its namesake. This gives the Trump brand unparalleled agility - in a networked global business environment that increasingly rewards agility.

3. Trump is a business-to-business brand, too, unlike almost all other luxury brands and iconic brands, which are overwhelmingly consumer-only brands. The Trump brand name enhances the Trump Organization's ability to open

doors and enter into real estate deals and licensing deals on highly advantageous terms, ones that yield low-risk high-return rewards.

When taken together, these three perspectives on the Trump brand show how the brand has only gotten stronger in the course of Trump's combative campaign for the presidency. Many commentators have marveled at Trump's refusal to moderate his views or "act more presidential" upon seizing the GOP nomination. But moderating his views would not only be an anathema to Trump personally, it would also severely undermine the values of bravery and non-conformity that the Trump brand stands for. Trump's brand essence is an extension of his outsized personality. To assume that Donald Trump would squelch that personality while ascending the biggest stage on earth – the U.S. presidential election – betrays an ignorance of both the man and the brand.

Trump, the Luxury Brand, Bold, Uncompromising and the Very Best!

As a luxury brand, the Trump brand plays by different rules than most other brands, which helps explain why no amount of "negative" publicity in the past has ever damaged the brand. Luxury brands don't need to be warm and well-behaved to be attractive and successful. Luxury brands are desirable because they are enviable.

This connection between envy and luxury brands was explored by marketer Chris Malone and social psychologist Susan B. Fiske in their book *The Human Brand*. The consumer brands we admire the most combine the qualities of "warmth and competence." Trusted consumer brands such as Campbell's, Hershey's and Johnson & Johnson all rank above average in consumer regard for their quality (competence) and in their positive intentions towards customers (warmth).

Luxury brands rate differently, however, in Malone and Fiske's studies. Mercedes, Porsche and Rolex are all highly regarded for their competence in terms of quality, but they are also rated low for "warmth." That's because the personality of luxury brands is one of taste and selectivity, not openness and friendliness.

Most people consider luxury brands to be exclusive, snobby and therefore cold. But that's also the source of their appeal. We envy their power and self-confidence and want to share in it. Luxury brands stand for quality products and turn their noses up at anyone unwilling to pay for them.

Now consider Donald Trump's famous saying from The Apprentice: "You're fired!" Every time he uttered that phrase with disgust on national television, he was burnishing the Trump brand image. Trump is a man and a brand so dedicated to his high standards that he's unafraid to fire people who don't measure up. Rather than pity the dismissed apprentices, TV viewers identified instead with the star of the show, the impatient, exasperated boss who accepts nothing but the best.

The reason why luxury brands tend to be so profitable is that consumers are willing to pay a premium to become a part of the select few. Consumers actually want to pay extra because paying extra assures them that they are in rarified company. Whenever luxury brands discount their prices, they do so very carefully and discreetly. Cutting prices can actually hurt a luxury brand's value in the long run.

This pricing philosophy is reflected in the Trump Organization's insistence on the "ultra-luxury" designation for its hotel properties. Ultra-luxury suggests you are getting a product that is beyond luxury – which gives a hotel enormous pricing power at a time when online travel sites are driving down room rates even at high-end hotels.

Trump has seized the GOP nomination and enhanced his personal fame by expressing the essence of the Trump ultra-luxury brand – one that's impatient with mediocrity, compromise, indecision and weakness. Buoyed by literally billions of dollars in free media during the presidential campaign, Trump has left an indelible image of a man and his brand that enviably does not settle for second-best. With more than 60 percent of voters believing the country is on the wrong track, they are open to Trump's claim that the country has been let down by politicians who lack such essential Trump brand attributes as dominance, courage and conviction.

Trump as an Iconic Brand

An icon (literally "image" in Greek) is a memorable image that stands for a simple, direct and powerful truth. An iconic brand is a brand that sells at a premium price because it offers its customers a stirring narrative that makes them happy to pay more to be a part of it.

Apple and Nike are classic iconic brands. There are cheaper cellphones and sneakers on the market, but Apple and Nike offer consumers something more for their dollars, a chance to be a part of their compelling brand narratives.

In this regard, Trump is unique in the world because the man and his iconic brand are one and the same. With his boisterous speaking style, aggressive demeanor and distinctive hairstyle, Trump casts a memorable image, one that is redolent of his brand narrative of boldness, certainty and indifference to convention.

In his 2004 book *How Brands become Icons*, Harvard professor Douglas B. Holt laid out for marketers these four essential steps for creating an iconic consumer brand. The similarities to the Trump brand are absolutely startling:

1. Target National Contradictions. Icons don't target consumer segments or psychographic types. They go after veins of intense anxieties and desires running through society.
2. Create Myths That Lead Culture. Unlike conventional branding, icons don't mimic pop culture; they lead it.
3. Speak with a Rebel's Voice. Icons don't seek to mirror the thoughts and emotions of their customers. They speak as rebels.
4. Draw on Political Authority to Rebuild the Myth. Icons don't behave as if they have to maintain a certain DNA or essential truth. They re-invent their myths and themselves.

In his book, Holt told of the difficulties that brand marketers have with all of these steps, especially item number four. Rebuilding or reshaping a brand's myth requires ordinary corporate managers to make the bold choice of stepping away from one myth and entering another – which is why so many iconic brands have trouble changing with the times. That difficulty puts a downward pressure on brand equity, because if the brand narrative or myth can't be sustained, brand value will decay over time.

This is yet another instance in which the Trump brand is unique. Trump is the physical embodiment of his own iconic brand. As such, he has shown an instinctive and unwavering ability to change his narrative, his mythology, as times change. Distinct from all the other brands in the world, the Trump can adjust, refresh and re-create his brand message and mythology just by speaking his mind. No other brand in the world enjoys such an advantage in keeping up with the public mood during these fast-moving times.

Back in 2015, political commentators with a shallow understanding of Trump and his brand wondered if the highly competitive Trump might quit the campaign after his first primary loss. Instead, each loss in a primary election gave Trump the chance to show off his natural talent for turning the narrative to suit his circumstances and set the stage for the next contest. As long as the narrative speaks through a rebel voice and addresses the anxieties and contradictions in the audience's minds, an iconic brand's narrative can turn any negative situation into a positive.

This was never more evident than in Trump's first stump speech, "I will build a wall." The media and mainstream politicians thought this was ludicrous and this immigration stance would kill Trump's chances. What happened was Trump's ratings soared and all the presidential candidates found it fashionable to talk about immigration.

Trump is Largely a Business-to-Business Brand

Although the Trump brand has a significant business-to-consumer component in the way it attracts condo buyers, hotel guests and consumers who purchase branded Trump products, the Trump brand is unique in that it enhances the Trump Organization's business-to-business dealings.

Donald Trump has always understood that fame creates power in the marketplace. He's understood that so well that he's even embraced so-called "negative" publicity as being a positive for his brand. Again, this is due to Trump's natural talent for handling publicity so that it aligns with his brand values of boldness, brazenness and indifference to convention. Whether the media was reporting his messy divorces or his companies in receivership, Trump made sure he never came off regretful, scared or worried. And so the reporting almost always helped make Trump more famous – the very image of a brave self-confident alpha male.

These and other Trump brand values, including quality, exclusivity, strength, certainty, and ultra-luxury play very strong among investors who wish to enhance their own status and prestige by association with the Trump brand. The presidential campaign is helping make Trump one of the most famous men on earth. In a world made small by social media and mobile connections, Trump commands a Midas touch of being able to project his thoughts and visions into this world at a moment's notice. The value of that level of fame, coupled with almost unparalleled access to media whenever he cares to speak, is very hard to value when it comes to attracting business partners or accessing the public markets for investment.

It is incalculable how much brand equity could be generated if Donald Trump should win the U.S. presidency and become the first celebrity billionaire in the White House. Losing the election, however, will also serve to build Trump's brand, because of Trump's well-documented ability to turn the narrative in his brand's favor. If he loses, don't be surprised to see him on CNN, Fox, CBS and just about every morning news program as a guest commenting on Hillary's decisions as president, all of which will continuously build his brand empire.

Having run the race claiming that his opponent is crooked, the media is slanted and the system is rigged, Trump's sizeable constituency will likely take his loss as further evidence that something is wrong with the country. Trump actually can win by losing, as he has many times in the past, because he never waivers from building his iconic brand around societal anxieties, cultural myths and his rebel's voice - the elements of iconic brand-building.

On the day after the November election, the Trump brand and its unique attributes will be stronger than ever – regardless of the vote tally from the night before. Win or lose, the story Trump tells the day after the election, will boost the value of his brand and make him more famous yet, because on that day, the whole world's attention will be focused on Donald J. Trump.

Unlocking the Brand Value

A luxury brand. An iconic brand. A business-to-business brand. All three of these factors point to a variety of attainable strategies necessary for fully realizing the $3.3 billion valuation of the Trump brand.

Put these three unique brand attributes together and add in world fame and virtually unlimited access to the media. It would take much more than $3.3 billion to try and build a branding juggernaut of that kind from scratch.

Work backward from that $3.3 billion estimate and there are countless ways that the full brand equity value of the Trump name can be realized in media properties, digital assets, consumer products, hotels, travel, recreation and luxury resorts. The question facing the Trump Organization is how to go about continuing to monetize the brand in different market segments in the coming years.

The clearest opportunity facing the Trump Organization today is to cultivate more connectivity among its various assets. By using new technologies to bring together luxury real estate, hospitality, travel, recreation and fine dining, the Trump name could become a global lifestyle brand that offers ultra-luxury experiences in every aspect of life.

Imagine a Trump Card that is so much more valuable than an American Express card, one which serves as your personal concierge, opening the door for you to club memberships, restaurant seating, golf course reservations, effortlessly taking you to the front of the line of wherever you want to go. A card that allows you hop into a rental car and gain access to a hotel room in any major city on earth. What would that be worth? How much would you pay for that?

The ecosystem economics of a Trump Card - or a key fob or a mobile phone app - could make the *Trump Experience* an exclusive and highly lucrative global luxury product. In competition with other luxury brands, the Trump Organization would have the edge in financing and execution because no other brand is so well-known and highly regarded for its commitment to luxury and exclusivity.

In expanding its portfolio of holdings, the one world-class business icon that the Trump Organization might take some tips from is Richard Branson and his *Virgin* brand. Not unlike Trump, Branson is a high-living, media-friendly, rule-breaking billionaire who operates largely on instinct and cunning. His Virgin Group Holdings, like the Trump Organization, is a holding company for varied interests, some of which are owned and controlled by Virgin and some of which only generate cash through licensing deals.

The brand values of Virgin are very different from Trump values, but the branding modus operandi is almost identical: Leverage the value of the brand for maximum returns with minimal risk. *Virgin Mobile* phones operate in the U.S. under a straight royalty agreement with Sprint. On the other hand, Virgin owns a 47 percent interest in *Virgin Money*, a financial services company in Great Britain.

The Virgin brand is so powerful in Great Britain that Branson's company took nearly half the equity in Virgin Money with no cash investment at all – it's share was paid for in brand equity alone. How do you calculate a multiple value for a brand like that? How do you calculate the rate of return on a zero-cash investment? Very few brands enjoy that kind of branding power, but Trump is one of them.

There is some concern among investors that the Virgin Group is so dependent on Richard Branson, at age 66, that the company will collapse as soon as he retires. Here is where the Trump brand has its fourth pillar of strength: the three Trump offspring responsible for running the Trump Organization. Although the years in which Donald Trump can continue to serve as the physical embodiment of his brand are limited, the brand's iconic status will undoubtedly contribute to its staying power.

In this respect, Trump resembles a historic brand icon who also held controversial political views: Henry Ford. More than 110 years after the company's founding, the *Ford* brand remains the strongest in the U.S. auto industry, with Henry Ford's great-grandson at the helm. Like the Ford brand, the Trump brand can live on as an extension of the founder's dominant and exacting personality. Because of the brand's emphasis on quality and luxury, the brand narrative has the power to transform itself repeatedly in the years to come. The immortal durability of Donald Trump's brand will likely prove to be the ultimate expression of *The Trump Factor*.

Donald Trump has over 10 million followers on both Facebook and Twitter and whether he wins or loses the presidential election he will arguably be one of the most famous men in the world. There is no other human being who can exploit his brand in such an influential manner – he has generated over $1 billion in free media – and commands market dominance, making the Trump brand virtually irreplaceable. Never in modern history has a candidate, in an election primary, filled arenas and coliseums for a political talk. In fact, many venues were sold out with standing room only.

Back in Emerald City, Toto pulled back the curtain and exposed the "Wizard" as a normal middle-aged man known as Professor Marvel. In this land of make-believe, the fantasy turned into reality as Dorothy woke up from her dream to learn that The Wizard of Oz never really existed.

That's not the case with Donald Trump, he is a human brand and his combined real estate holdings and brand equity are worth far more than most media outlets are reporting. While the brand component is subjective, there is no doubt that the valuation is worth much more than Bloomberg's mere $35 million estimate (Trump could sell his email list for that much).

To be honest, when I started writing this book over three years ago, I would have never guessed that the Trump brand would be worth over $3 billion, yet the presidential hopeful has proven that he can move markets and his legacy as a tough dealmaker will go down in the record books. The pipeline for Trump-branded real estate is stronger than ever and I have little doubt that the Trump family will continue to exploit its most precious intellectual property, American success.

We're now at the end of the road and it is time to expose the true net worth of Donald J. Trump. All of the mysteries have now been converted to math and based upon all of the facts and resources available, which I spent three years working with, the research indicates the billionaire is worth an estimated $9.366 billion.

The research to support this valuation cannot be disputed. The logic for this calculation is sound. The experts in their field of valuation were called upon for this book and are the best in their respective industries.

No doubt the media will try to poke holes in this valuation claiming it is too high and not based on facts, yet after presenting the evidence, research and logic in this book, you will have to decide if you are swayed by me or the media. Ben Graham famously wrote *Security Analysis*,

"Have the courage of your knowledge and experience. If you have formed a conclusion from the facts and if you know your judgment is sound, act on it—even though others may hesitate or differ."

In full disclosure, I wrote this book on my own, financed my research and drew my own conclusions with no influence or persuasion from anyone. My book is an honest look at a corporate icon and it's an unbiased analyst's perspective on Donald Trump's wealth accumulation, including his brand.

When Donald Trump, along with Tony Schwartz, wrote *The Art of the Deal* in 1988, they were paid to publish a book that became a smashing success - over 3 million copies sold to date – according to *Forbes* in 2014. The book broke records and has continued to fly off the shelf because people want to know the secrets for American success.

I told Donald Trump over three years ago that I was going to write a book that would be, in my words, the sequel to *The Art of the Deal*. I also told him that my book would be better. He looked at me, smiled, and said "good luck." You be the judge. I hope you enjoyed reading *The Trump Factor: Unlocking the Secrets Behind the Trump Empire.*

SOURCES

Introduction
Exposing the Wonderful Wizard of Trump

1. *Philosiblog.com*, 2012. Dorothy in *The Wizard of Oz*, quote, Pg 1

Chapter 1
The Raised Nail Gets Hammered

1. Abelson, M., 2015. *Bloomberg, How Trump Invented Trump*, Pg 7
2. Buettner, R., and Bagli, C.V., 2015. *The New York Times*, quote, Pg 7 (June ed.)
3. Jim Rohn, *GoodReads.com*, entrepreneur, author, quote Pg 4-5
4. Jonathan Laing, *Barron's, Trump's Blustery 1990 Campaign Against a Wall Street Analyst*, quote Pg 7-8
5. O'Harrow, R., 2016. *The Washington Post*, quote Pg 8 (Jan. ed.)
6. *Politico*, 2015. Joel Ross, Investment Banker, quote Pg 8 (July ed.)
7. *The Economist* 2016. Quote Pg 8 (Feb. ed.)
8. Warren Buffett, *GoodReads.com,* and *BrainyQuote.com*, CEO Berkshire Hathaway, quote Pg 4
9. Wheeler, L., 2015. *Trump Gets Heated With Chris Wallace*, quotes Pg 8
10. Zig Ziglar, *BrainyQuote.com*, investment writer, quote Pg 5

Chapter 2
The Fifth Avenue Crown Jewel

1. Blair, Gwenda, 2015. *Donald Trump, The Candidate*, Jan A. d'Alessio *quote*, Pg 12

2. *Bloomberg*, 2016. *Trump is Richer in Property and Deeper in Debt in New Valuation, (2016-07-19*) reference to Trump Tower refinancing (3) Pg17

3. Gray, C., editor, *The New York Times The Store that Slipped Through the Cracks*, Pg 11

4. *Louis Sunshine.com*, Donald Trump's first real estate salesperson quote, Pg 13

5. Marino, V., *The New York Times*, 2013. *Arthur W. Zeckendorf, a 30-Minute Interview*, Pg 15

6. *New York Archives*, 2016. *The Political Fate of Bonwit Teller*, Joseph Kaminski quote, Pg 11

7. Ross, G., 2006. *Trump Strategies for Real Estate: Billionaire Lessons for the Small Investor*, Pg 13, quote regarding the naming of Trump Tower, (4) Pg 17

8. *The Chicago Tribune*, 1994. *A bigger Niketown: The Trump Organization Said Tuesday it* . . . article regarding Nike, reference to Nike square footage (1) and reference to Trump regarding Nike (2), Pg 16

9. Trump, D., 2008. *Trump Never Give Up: How I Turned My Biggest Challenges Into Successes*, Pg 12

10. Trump, D., and Schwartz, T., 2015. *The Art of the Deal*, Pg 11

11. Trump, D., and Swartz, T., 2009. *The Art of the Deal*, Consolo, F.H., Chairman of Retail Leasing, quote, also D. Elliman, Real Estate, quote Pg 16

12. Wooten, S, 2008. *From Real Estate to Reality TV*, a *New York Times*, 1979, article quote (July 1, 1979) Pg 15

13. Trump, D., and Swartz, T., 2009. *The Art of the Deal*, Consolo, F.H., Chairman of Retail Leasing, quote, also D. Elliman, Real Estate, quote Pg 13

14. Wooten, S, 2008. *From Real Estate to Reality TV*, a *New York Times*, 1979, article quote (July 1, 1979) Pg 12

Chapter 3
Trump's Wall Street Piggy Bank

1. *Bloomberg, L.P., 2016. Trump is Richer in Property and Deeper in Debt in New Valuation*, Pg 26
2. Chandan, S., PhD, Associate Dean at *NYU's Schack Institute of Real Estate,* Pg 26
3. Costello, J., *Real Capital Analytics* (RCA) Real Estate Service, quote, Pg 25
4. Kusisto, L., 2012. *The Wall Street Journal, 40 Wall Fortunes Rise Again*, Trump quote on Kinson Company, Pg 24
5. Kusisto, L., 2012. *The Wall Street Journal, Forty Wall Fortune Rises Again*, Trump, D., Jr., quote, Pg 22
6. Rockefeller, J.D., *Brainyquote.com*, Industrialist, quote, Pg 19
7. *The Wall Street Journal*, 2012. *40 Wall Fortune's Rise Again*, article on tenant lawsuit with Jeffrey Lichtenberg, of Cushman & Wakefield, the landlord's agent, Pg 25
8. Trump, D., and Bohner, J., 1997. *Trump: The Art of the Comeback*, Pg 20

Chapter 4
The Often Overlooked Trophies

1. Bagli, C., *Chicago Tribune*, 2002. *Partnership in Deal for Empire State Building*, Pg 32
2. *Bloomberg (2016-07-19), 2016. Trump is Richer in Property and Deeper in Debt in New Valuation*, Pg 29
3. *The New York Times*, 2002. *Quote re:* John Moore, Trump Parc building tenant, Pg 32
4. *The Real Deal, New York Real Estate News*. 2015. *Steve Roth on How He Made It*, Founder, Chairman, and CEO of Vornado Realty Trust (NYSE: VNO), Pg 31
5. Trump, D., and Schwartz, T., 2015. *The Art of the Deal*, Pg 28
6. *Vanity Fair*, 1987. *Big Deal, How I Do It My Way*. on the central park properties, *The Art of the Deal*, excerpt Pg 33

Chapter 5
Trump Hotels

1. Blair, G., 2000. *The Trumps: Three Generations That Built an Empire.* Pg 37
2. *BrainyQuote.com,* Hilton, C., hotelier, Pg 36
3. Cuozzo, S., *New York Post,* 2016. *How Donald Trump helped save New York City,* Pg 38
4. *Friedrich Drumpf and Family,* 2015. *Donald Trump Inherited More Than Just Cash from Immigrant Grandfather, as Some of NYC's Most Wealthiest Wills Revealed,* 2015. Pg 36-37
5. *Goodreads.com,* Graham, B., investor, quote, Pg 40
6. Hirsh, M., 2015. *How Debt Tamed Donald,* Pgs 39-40
7. *JDeRoos.com,* deRoos, J., Ph.D., HVS Professor of Hotel Finance and Real Estate at Cornell University, quote, Pg 44
8. Pogrebin, R., 1996. *The New York Times, 52-Story comeback is so Very Trump; Columbus Circle Tower Proclaims that Modesty is an Overrated Issue,* quotes, Pg 41
9. Ross, G., Executive Vice President and Senior Counsel,2006. *Trump Strategies for Real Estate: Billionaire Lessons for the Small Investor,* Pg 38
10. *The New York Times,* 2013. *Interview with Arthur W. Zeckendorf,* (1) Pg 37

Chapter 6
Trump International Hotel and Tower Chicago

1. *Belief.net,* Trump, quote, Pg 46
2. *Pursuitist.com, Trump Tower Penthouse Sells for $17 Million Making it Chicago's Most Expensive Residential Sale,* Shah, S., Founder and CEO of Vistex, quote Pg 47, 48
3. *The Chicago Tribune,* 2014. *Trump Tower Chicago Review* and *Trump Tower Represents Concrete Feat,* http://articles. chicagotribune.com/keyword/trump-tower, also reference to Mayor Daley's *Landscape Awards,* press release, quote, Pg 47
4. Trump's Federal Election Campaign *(FEC) filings,* Pg 51

Chapter 7
Trump International Las Vegas

1. Barbieri, K., 2015. *Ruffin Reveals the Secrets of Running a Billion Dollar Empire*, Pg 56
2. *Biography*, articles and quote, Klein, H., former V.P. at Trump Taj Mahal, Pg 57
3. *Forbes*, 2014. *#722 Phillip Ruffin*, reference to Vegas deal Carl Ichan, Yitzhak Tshuva, and Phil Ruffin, Pg 54
4. *Las Vegas Review-Journal*. 2015. *Treasure Island Owner Says MGM Resorts Rejected the 1.3 Billion Offer for the Mirage*, Pg 56
5. Simpson, J., and Ridder, K., 2003. *The Chicago Tribune, Trump's Got Even Bigger Plans for Las Vegas Project*, quote, Pg 53
6. *The Las Vegas Sun, An Empire Built on Assets, Not Debt*, quote, Pg 55
7. Wenzl, R, and Heying, T., 2010. *The Wichita Eagle, A Comfortable Fit for Phil Ruffins Billions*, Phil Ruffin, Businessman, quote, Pg 55

Chapter 8
Trump International Hotel Washington DC

1. *Biography*, Kroc, R., businessman, philanthropist, quote, Pg 60
2. *JDeRoos.com*, deRoos, J., Ph.D., HVS Professor of Hotel Finance and Real Estate at Cornell University, published journal aricles, Pg 67, 69

Chapter 9
Magnificient Mar-a-Lago

1. *Biography*, Coco Chanel, quote, Pg 72
2. *Biography*, Taubman, B., CEO of *Taubman Centers*, quote, Pg 79
3. Blair, G., 2000.*The Trumps: Three Generations That Built an Empire*, Pg 75
4. Jordan, M., and Helderman, R., 2015. *The Washington Post, Inside Trump's Palm Beach Castle and His 30 Year Fight to Win Over the Locals*, Jane Day, Palm Beach historic preservation consultant, quote, Pg 78

5. Keneally, M., 2016. Inside Donald Trump's Mar-A-Lago Estate, Where He's 'Done So Much for Equality', Pg 72

6. Newman, M, 2009. *Donald's Digs in Palm Beach: Mar-a-Lago*, Lembcke, B., Executive VP, Managing Director of Trump Properties, quote, Pg 80

7. *Pursuitist.com*, 2016. *10 Things to Know about Mar-a-Lago, Donald Trump's Palm Beach Estate*, re: Forbes reference to 1985 and 1989 and *Town and Country Magazine*, 2016. *A History of Mar-a-Lago, Donald Trump's American Castle*, 2016. Quote, Pg 72, 73

8. Qui, L., 2015. *Is Donald Trump's Art of the Deal the Best-Selling Business Book of All Time?*, Pg 71

9. Salibury, S., 1992, *The Sun-Sentinel, Mansion Muddle, Financial Woes Leave Mar-a-Lago With Uncertain future*, former Palm Beach attorney, Paul Rampell, quote, Pg 78-79

10. Salisbury, S. 1992. *Mansion Muddles Financial Woes Leave Mar-a-Lago with Uncertain Future*, Pg 73

11. Singer, M., 2011, *Best Wishes Donald, The New Yorker*, quote, Pg 76

12. Trump, D., 2004. *Think Like a Billionnaire*, Pg 77, 79

13. Trump, D., and Bohner, J., 1997. *Trump: The Art of the Comeback*, Pg 74, 76

14. Trump, D., and McIver, M., 2008, *Trump Never Give Up: How I Turned My Biggest Challenges in Success*, Pg 76-77

15. Trump's Federal Election Commission *(FEC) filings* dated 7-15-15, Pg 79

Chapter 10
Trump is the "Four Seasons Hotel Chain" of Golf

1. Demby, R., *The Semi- Annual Golf & Resort Investment Report*, 2012 and 2013 and 2015 Years in Review. www.leisurepropertiesgroup.com, Pg 87

2. Ekovich, S., National Managing Director and First Vice President of the *Leisure Investment Properties Group* for Marcus and Millichap, golf real estate statistics, Pg 82-89

3. Ewan, D., 2011. *Chasing Paradise, Donald Trump and the Battle for the World's Greatest Golf Course*, Pg 90

4. Kilgannon, C., 2002. *The New York Times, Development: The Course that Trump Built,* Pg 89

5. *The National Golf Foundation,* (NGF) golf data, Pgs 86, 88, 89

Chapter 11
Trump Golf

1. *AlvinAlexander.com,* Gary Player, quote, Pg 92

2. Baratko, T., 2016. *Trump Says His Louden Golf Course is Worth $50M, County Assessors Say Less,* Pg 95

3. Barton, J., 2014. *Golf Digest, Donald Trump: I'm Huge!* interview, Pg 92

4. Donald Trump's *New York Military Academy Yearbook,* 1960, Pg 92

5. Ewan, D., 2011. *Chasing Paradise, Donald Trump and the Battle for the World's Greatest Golf Course,* Pg 91

6. *Golf Digest,* 2015 and 2016. *Golf Digest Magazines, Americas 100 Greatest Golfcourses,* Golf rankings, Pg 95

7. *Golf Magazine,* 2005. *World's 100 Greatest Golf Courses,* Golf rankings, Pg 95

8. *Golf Magazine, Our Story-Trump Golf,* Pg 94

9. *Golf.com, Donald Trump: King of Clubs,* interview, Pg 92-93

10. *GolfInc Magazine, Trump Buys Ritz-Carlton in Jupiter,* Trump quote, Pg 100

11. Jim Fazio, designer, *Trump International Palm Beach website,* quote, Pg 94

12. Kiefer, P., 2010. *The Real Deal, Developers See Golf Club Troubles, and Start Buying,* Trump, E., Executive Vice President of Development and Acquisitions, quote, Pg 97

13. Kilgannon, C., 2002. *The New York Times, Development: The Course that Trump Built,* Pg 91

14. *Music Television* (MTV) 2010. Reference to Red Sox, Pg 92

15. Sullivan, W., *The Star-Ledger,* 2008, *Trump Adds Shadow Isle in Colt's Neck to His Club,* (3) Pg 98

16. *The Los Angeles Times,* 2002. *Trump's Risks and Riches Par for the Course,* on Ocean Trails golf course, (1) Pg 96

17. Thomas, B., 2013. *Trump Tees Up Another a Tee in Scotland*, quote, Pg 92

18. *Variety*, 2016. *Donald Trump's Palos Verdes Golf Course Has Holes In It (Exclusive)*, Pg 92

19. Wright, K., *Donald Trump Opens New Tennis Center in Sterling*, 2015. Pg 95

Chapter 12
Doral: A Diamond in the Rough

1. Ackerman, J., 2014. *Inside Look at Gary Player Villa at Trump National Doral*, quote, Pg 104

2. Babineau, J., *The Sentinel* Staff, quote, Pg 106

3. Burke, M., *Forbes*, 2013. *How Ivanka Trump Got the Doral (and the Blue Monster) for a Bargain Basement Price and Had a Baby at the Same Time*, Ivanka Trump, businesswoman, model, quote, 107-108

4. Gray, W. 2016. *Tour Moving Doral Tournament to Mexico City*, Pg 110

5. Passov, J. 2015. *Golf.com, Donald Trump on Golf and Goals*, (1) Pg 110

6. *South Florida Business Journal*, 2012. *Trump Closes Doral Resort Deal*, Trump, D., quotes, Pg 110

7. U, H., and Levitt, D, 2011. *Paulson Group Said to Seize CNL Hotels from Morgan Stanley Funds, Bloomberg, L.P.*, 2011. Quote, Pg 106

Chapter 13
The Scottish Dealmaker

1. *'I Feel Scottish' Says Donald Trump on Flying Visit to Mother's Cottage*, Maryanne Trump Barry, Senior US Circuit Judge, Trump's sister, quote, Pg 113

2. Baxter, A., filmmaker, 2011. *You've Been Trumped*, Pg 115

3. *Brainyquote.com*, Sean Connery, quote, 112

4. *BusinessWire*, 2008. *Berkshire Hathaway, Starwood Completes Sale of Iconic of Turnberry Resort in Scotland to Leisurecorp*, Rogers, A., Group-CEO, Leisurecorp, quote, Pg 118

5. Cable, S, 2014. *Top Trumps! Donald Trump's Golf Resort Awarded Five-Star Status By Scottish Tourism Chiefs After US Tycoon Spends Millions Restoring Historic Mansion*, Sarah Malone, CEO, Aberdeen, quotes, (2) Pg 116-117

6. Carrell, S., 2010. *Filmmakers Arrested on Site of Scottish Golf Resort*, George Sorial, Trump attorney, *Biography*, quote, 115

7. *Condé Nast Traveler,2015. Top 30 Resorts in Europe, Readers' Choice Awards, 2015, and Travel + Leisure*, articles rating the Scotland course, Pg 120

8. *Daily Mail UK* website, *Stornoway Gazette* story, Pg 112

9. *Deadspin.com*, 2012. Quote, Pg 117 (1)

10. Federal Election Campaign *Filings*, data regarding value, Pg 121

11. *Golf.com*, 2014. *Wells Fargo Championship Leaderboard 2014 Results Prompt Scores Today*, quote, Pg 119

12. *No Love Lost in Lewis for Trump's Scotish Roots*, Deutsche Welle website, family data, Pg 113

13. Owen, D., *Golf Digest, Trump World*, quote, Pg 114, 115

14. *Scottish Roots.com, Donald Trump*, Pg 112

15. *The Independent* in London, 2014. *Donald Trump Buys Famed Turnberry Course in Scotland; Links Course Has Hosted Open 3 Times, 2014*, (3) Pg 119

16. *Twitter.com*, 2014. Trump tweet, quote, Pg 113

17. Wilkinson, D, 2012. *Trump Opens Controversial $150M Golf Course in Scotland, Golf World Magazine*, quote, Pg 115

Chapter 14
Trump Toys

1. *Brainyquote.com,* Trump, D., quote, Pg 124

2. *CNBC*, 2015. *Super Lives of the Super Rich* in a segment entitled "*Pimp My Chopper.*" Pg 128

3. Craig, S., 2016. *The New York Times, Donald Trump's Aging Air Fleet Gives His Bid and His Brand a Lift,. Donald Trump's Private Air Force One Documentary*, Pg 128

4. *Forbes*, 2011. *John Kluge 2011 Billionaires Drop Off List*, regarding 1989 and 2008 net worth of Kluge and home, (1) Pg 129-130
5. *Kashino, M., 2015. The Washingtonian, The Greatest, Most Amazing, Absolutely Huge Story of How Donald Trump Took Over Virginia's Biggest Vineyard*, Eric Trump quote, Pg 131
6. Kenny Rogers in *The Gambler*, quote, Pg 126
7. Linh, D., 1991. *Reuters, Debt Ridden Donald Trump Lost His 'Ship of Jewels' to a Saudi Prince*, Trump quote, Pg 125
8. *McKenzie, S., 2015. The $1 Billion SuperYacht: Bigger, Longer, But is it Better? The Los Angeles Times*, quote, Pg 124-125
9. *Pittsburg Post-Gazette*, 2016. Roth, E., aircraft interior designer, quote, Pg 128
10. Rappeport, A., 2015. *The New York Times, Looking Back at Donald Trump's 2015*, regarding Bedford home, Pg 132
11. Smithsonian Channel's *Mighty Planes*, John Dunkin, Trump's pilot, quote, Pg 127
12. Traugott, T., author of wine blog *Charlottesville Uncorked*, Pg 131
13. Trump, D., and Leerhsen, C., 1990. *Surviving at the Top*, excerpt in chapter "*Ship of Jewels*", Pg 125
14. Trump, D., and Schwartz, T., 2015. *The Art of the Deal*, Pg 123
15. *Turnberry Resort's website, http://www.trumpturnberry.com/ helicopter*, Pg 129

Chapter 15
A Blueprint Worth Billions

1. CNN Money, John D. Rockefeller, *The Richest Americans in History*, 2014.
2. Lowenstein, R., 2008. *Buffett: The Making of an American Capitalist*, Roger Lowenstein, financial journalist and writer, quote, Pg 134-135
3. Melby, C. and Rubin, R., 2015. *Here's Our Tally of Donald Trump's Wealth, The Bloomberg Billionaire Index*, regarding Trump's net worth, Pg 137, 138

4. *Obituary Financiers Fortune in Oil Amassed in Industrial Era of 'Rugged Individualism, The New York Times*, 1937, quote on Rockefeller, Pg 134

5. Scaramucci, A., 2016. *The Entrepreneur's Case for Trump*, quotes, Pg 136

6. Schroeder, A., 2009. *Wall Street Journal, Warren Buffet and the Business Life*, quote, Pg 136

7. Stibel, Jeff, 2014. *Warren Buffett: A Profile in Failure*, featured in: Banking & Finance, Leadership & Management

8. *The Definitive Net Worth of Donald Trump, 2015. Forbes*, regarding Trump's net worth, Pg 137, 138

9. *The Dynasties, 2002. Forbes*, details on Rockefeller, (1) Pg 134

10. Thomas, B., 2013. *How to Pick REIT Stocks Like Trump and Think Like Graham*, and Warren Buffett, investor and philanthropist, regarding extreme conservatism, quote, Pg 135

11. Thomas, B., 2015. *It's Time to be a Greedy REIT Investor*, Sir John Templeton, stock investor, quote, Pg 136

12. Tully, S., 2016. *Here's How Much Donald Trump's Net Worth Jumped in the Last 10 Months, Fortune*, regarding Trump's net worth, Pg 137, 138

13. *Values.com*, John D Rockefeller, quote, Pg 134

14. Williams, F.,1930. *If You Must Speculate, Learn The Rules*, Pg 134

Chapter 16
The Trump Brand

1. *Bloomberg Business Week*, 2016. Brand valuation, Pg 142

2. Holt, D., 2004. *How Brands become Icons*, Pg 145

3. Holt, D., 2013 *How to Build Iconic Brands*, slideshare Pg 142-143

4. Malone, C., Fiske, S., and Runnette, S., 2014. *The Human Brand*, Pg 143

5. *Predictiv*. 2011. Brand valuation, Pg 142

6. The Wizard of Oz, quote, Pg150

7. VintageValueInvesting.com, 2016. *Ben Graham's 4 Guiding Business Principles*, Pg 150

ABOUT THE AUTHOR

Brad Thomas is a leading commercial real estate analyst and editor of the *Forbes Real Estate Investor* (monthly newsletter). As a former developer, Thomas understands the complexities of planning, design, construction, and finance–all essential ingredients to value creation.

He is also a prolific writer having appeared in *Forbes, MarketWatch, Institutional Investor,* and *The Street.* Thomas is currently the #1 writer on Seeking Alpha where his articles generate over 3 million annual page views.

Thomas is also the co-author of *The Intelligent REIT Investor* (Wiley) and he is a consultant to Aurus, a Latin American Asset Manager based in Santiago. Thomas graduated from Presbyterian College in Clinton, South Carolina.

CONTRIBUTING RESEARCH ANALYSTS

Jonathan Morris
Adjunct Professor, Georgetown University

Mr. Morris is a seasoned commercial real estate executive with over 25 years of experience working for top tier companies. He is a leading expert on real estate investment trusts (REITs) and he has held responsible senior executive and partner positions for many blue chip companies such as Boston Properties, Director of Acquisitions; Charles E. Smith (Archstone-Smith), Director of Acquisitions; Lerner Enterprises affiliate LMH Realty Group LLC, Partner; and Rosecliff Realty, EVP, COO and Managing Director, Capital Markets (Rosecliff was owned by Brown Brothers Harriman).

Morris is a native of Washington, D.C. where he has been a celebrated professor at Georgetown University. He teaches in the Master of Real Estate program. His unique course includes frequent guest speakers and focuses on the public REIT sector (Morris teaches out of a textbook titled *The Intelligent REIT Investor* which is co-authored by Brad Thomas and Stephanie Krewson-Kelly).

Morris is a graduate of Towson University which he attended on a track scholarship. He also studied for his MBA at George Washington University in Washington, D.C.

Steven M. Ekovich
First Vice President, Director National Golf Division
Leisure Investment Properties Group

Mr. Ekovich has been in the real estate business since 1985, both brokering commercial real estate and serving as Regional Manager for several Marcus & Millichap offices. He has closed or overseen over $4 billion of real estate transactions. Currently Ekovich is the National Managing Director of the Leisure Investment Properties Group and Vice President of Investments for Marcus & Millichap.

Since 2011 Mr. Ekovich has listed, sold and underwritten in excess $2.5 billion of golf and golf & resort properties, in addition to selling 85 golf assets. Ekovich has sold golf courses, golf resorts and golf master planned communities for the nation's largest banking institutions, as well as major national and international golf asset owners.

Ekovich has been a published author in numerous golf trade publications such as *Golf Inc.*, *Golf Business*, and *Florida Golf Central* and has been named one of the top ten "Movers & Shakers" by *Golf Business* for 2014, 2015 and 2016. Additionally, Ekovich is routinely called upon for golf industry statistics and quotes by well-known institutions such as *Bloomberg News*, *The New York Times* and the *Business Journals* in major metropolitan areas and was spotlighted on Bryant Gumble's HBO Real Sports in 2014. He has been a featured speaker since 1998 at real estate and golf industry events nationally.